KING
ARTHUR

POCKET
GIANTS

KING
ARTHUR

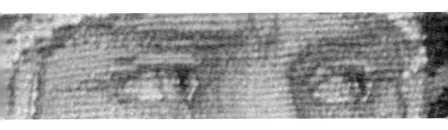

POCKET
GIANTS

NICK
HIGHAM

The History Press

For Cheryl

First published 2015

The History Press
The Mill, Brimscombe Port
Stroud, Gloucestershire, GL5 2QG
www.thehistorypress.co.uk

British Library Cataloguing in Publication Data.
A catalogue record for this book is available from the British Library.

ISBN 978 0 7509 5921 6

Typesetting and origination by The History Press
Printed in Malta by Melita Press.

Contents

Acknowledgements

Over the years I have been privileged to discuss King Arthur with very many scholars, far too numerous to mention here, but to all my grateful thanks. My particular thanks go to Professor John Colarusso, who generously allowed me access to his translation of the Ossetian Nart Sagas prior to their publication, and corresponded with me on several issues; and to Dr Luca Larpi, who read and commented on a draft of the text. I am grateful, too, to Tony Morris, as series editor, the staff of The History Press, and Jessica Cuthbert-Smith, as copy editor, for seeing the book through to publication. All errors remain my own responsibility. Above all, my thanks go to my wife, Cheryl, to whom this book is dedicated with love.

1

The Greatness of Arthur

'Camelot–Camelot,' said I to myself. 'I don't seem to remember hearing of it before. Name of the asylum, likely'.

Mark Twain, 1889[1]

A recently published ranking of the most significant people in history gives the top three spots to Jesus, Napoleon and Muhammad.[2] Checking these against web hits early in 2014 produced 48 million for Christ, 44 million for Muhammad but only 6 million for Napoleon. Popularity in these terms can indicate many different things, of course, but type in 'King Arthur' and over 45 million internet sites are listed. Clearly, few figures from the past excite more interest. And this is not unique to the online world, for the number of books in which Arthur's name appears in the title is similarly exceptional. Also, unlike such notables as Adolf Hitler (number seven in the above rankings), Arthur is generally remembered positively, as a good ruler who led his people wisely and presided over a golden age. As 'the once and future king' who will come again to rescue his people, Arthur even parallels Jesus as a saviour; many 'Arthurian' tales contain a spiritual and pastoral message. He is often portrayed as protective of the weak and hard on wrongdoers. Tales of Arthur are both edifying and uplifting. They form part of the universal struggle between 'good' and 'evil'.

But who we think Arthur was, and what he represents, has shifted repeatedly across the centuries, moving backwards and forwards between myth, legend and history.

Throughout the Middle Ages he was a subject for ecclesiastical authors as much as courtly writers, folk tales alongside popular romances. His story wove together old themes with new exploits and comrades, as different writers told his tale for different reasons to different audiences. In this sense there are a multitude of Arthurs, coalescing and dividing repeatedly over time.

How old is Arthur's story? Some locate its origins in Ancient Greece or the Near East. Others look to the Roman Empire as its epicentre, even from as far away as the Black Sea. In the Christian era, however, he is generally located primarily in Britain and most people today think of Arthur as rooted in British (i.e. Welsh, Cornish and Breton) folklore and storytelling. The victorious and ostentatiously Christian warrior fighting against pagan barbarian invaders first emerges in the *History of the Britons*, written in Wales in the early ninth century.[3] It is here that the Arthur of the medieval storytellers was born – though he was not yet a king, simply a great warrior. Kingship was conferred in Welsh literature dating possibly from the tenth century and more certainly from the eleventh and twelfth, though it is difficult to tell how long oral stories featuring Arthur as a king had been circulating by this point.

This Celtic Arthur had no appeal for Anglo-Saxon authors, representing as he did their opponents for the control of Britain. The Norman Conquest, however, brought about a dramatic shake-up of cultural values, downgrading the 'Saxons' or English, who had previously dominated the story of Britain, in favour of their earlier opponents. There are signs of a new interest in Arthur soon after: he appears, for example, looking very like a mounted Norman knight of the day, on vaulting in the cathedral in Modena (north Italy) built between about 1090 and 1120, with the inscription *Artus de Bretani* above. But Arthur's fame was really kick-started in the mid-1130s by Geoffrey of Monmouth, who wrote a very different history to the one enshrined, for example, in Bede's works or in the *Anglo-Saxon Chronicle*. Geoffrey developed an idea first found in the *History of the Britons* that the Britons were descendants of the Trojans, and he contrived a pseudo-history centred on their activities in Britain. He followed their fortunes there for a millennium or more. King Arthur was central to Geoffrey's *History of the Kings of Britain*, a great overlord, the conqueror of other kings and their peoples in the British Isles and across much of the Western world.[4]

Geoffrey's work was very poor history, but it was a huge bestseller by the standards of the day. Arthur's story mushroomed across Europe as a result, reaching even as far afield as the Holy Land. A mass of literature developed, particularly in France and Germany, spreading outwards into virtually every European language. Glastonbury Abbey quickly claimed his grave; Richard the Lionheart gave what was supposedly Arthur's sword to one of his German allies on crusade in the 1190s.

As a late twelfth-century French writer put it, at about the time when the crusader kingdom of Jerusalem was coming to an end and when refugees from the Frankish East were to be found everywhere in Europe: 'Whither has not flying fame spread and familiarised the name of Arthur

Cadbury, and the Roman historian John Morris.[8] Both rewrote the history of Dark Age Britain, centring it on Celtic or sub-Roman 'British' culture as opposed to that of the 'Germanic' Anglo-Saxons. At the core of each account was a great king who held together the old Roman rule for a generation and threw back the invading Saxons by force of arms. Arthur returned to our histories in a blaze of glory, which has never since quite died away.

Across the twentieth century and into the twenty-first, Arthur has also featured widely in novels, musicals and plays, on television and in film. When the Monty Python team turned their attention to movie-making, they started with *Monty Python and the Holy Grail* (1975), since adapted as the comedy musical *Spamalot*, which opened on Broadway in 2005. There have been over fifty feature films based on Arthurian stories since the first in 1904. Every schoolchild knows his name, and most could add other details: Arthur ruled at Camelot, for example; his wife was Guinevere; his sword was Excalibur; he drew the sword from the stone and led the knights of the Round Table. Even the names of some of his knights – Galahad, Gawain, Lancelot, Kay – are widely remembered. Arthurian terms have entered our everyday vocabulary: today we still pursue the 'Holy Grail', and hold 'round table' discussions.

Once you start looking, Arthur is everywhere. In the UK, Camelot runs the National Lottery. In the US the same name is associated with the Kennedy White House – based on the President's penchant for the musical *Camelot*, first performed in 1960 then made into a film in 1964, shortly after his assassination in November 1963. The Queen's robing room at the Houses of Parliament was decorated with Arthurian carvings by William Dyce in Victoria's reign. Seventy-four locomotives of the so-called 'King Arthur class' were built in the UK between 1919 and 1926. Today the steam locomotives *King Arthur*, *Merlin*, *Excalibur* and *Pendragon* power the narrow-gauge Rudyard Lake Steam Railway in Staffordshire; *Mordred* is the petrol loco. King Arthur Flour is a US company established in 1790 and still flourishing; Excalibur is a simulation games publisher. Arthur even gives his name to part of a mathematical theorem: Talbot's Theorem of King Arthur and his Knights of the Round Table.

King Arthur's giant presence in our culture is assured. There is, however, something distinctive and different about him. For, while we are in a position to offer a life story, with dates, for almost all the other figures featured in the Pocket GIANTS series, and to discuss their impact on their world, we can have no confidence in any particular outline of Arthur's life, his family connections or his deeds. We do not know precisely where he lived or when. Indeed, there is doubt as to whether or not a *real* 'King Arthur' lived at all. There may have been numerous different Arthurs whose stories have been woven together. Or perhaps the whole 'King Arthur' phenomenon is no more than storytelling, allowing the generation and regeneration of tales by a succession of commentators, each developing, reinforcing but changing a common legend. There is a danger that we are writing about a character who is essentially fictional.

Such doubts about the very existence of King Arthur make this short book very different to one on, say, Alexander the Great, or Julius Caesar. Instead of telling his life story and analysing his place in history, we must explore where, when and why various different King Arthurs emerged. The focus of this book is therefore not only on a single individual, but also on the various authors who wrote about him. It explores the purposes he served in their reimaginings of the past, and the values enshrined in the stories which repeatedly drew writers and audiences back to him.

There are many books about the 'historical' Arthur. Most have serious weaknesses. Their authors use evidence which is at best ambiguous, at worst inelig ible. They often write without the skills of the historian, the linguist and the archaeologist which are necessary for a balanced interpretation. They pile hypothesis upon hypothesis to build a veritable house of cards. There seems to be a virtually insatiable readership for such material (which is a significant phenomenon in itself).[9] But in a pocket-sized book like this, there is no space to examine these accounts individually, and collectively they are best set aside as unhelpful or, at least, unhistorical.[10]

This still leaves us with our central questions. Who was King Arthur? Can we establish enough about him to consider him historical? Or should we think of him as a character of myth or legend? I propose to follow the trail chronologically, assessing the strengths and weaknesses of several very different theories. We will begin our journey in antiquity and end in the present. Along the way I hope what we do and do not know about Arthur becomes clearer.

2

Arthur in Antiquity

The themes in question originated in an area remote from the Mediterranean and arrived in northern Britain almost three centuries before the legendary Arthur rode over the British countryside with his knights. These legends were then imprinted by specific historical events that occurred in Late Antiquity, the major participants in which were the dramatically displaced tribes of Sarmatians and Alans who found themselves settled in Britain and Gaul.

C. Scott Littleton and Linda A. Malcor, 2000[11]

The quest for King Arthur extends far beyond the shores of Britain and goes back long before the Dark Ages. It begins with his name. In the 1920s, the American scholar Kemp Malone suggested a link with inscriptions found in Roman Dalmatia (now Croatia) which summarise the career of a certain Lucius Artorius Castus.[12] The anthropologist C. Scott Littleton and, more recently, Linda Malcor have taken Kemp's suggestion much further. They highlight similarities between Arthurian stories and folk tales from the region of Ossetia in the mountains of the Caucasus, arguing that these tales were originally brought to the West in the Roman period by Sarmatian and Alan cavalry, ancestors of the modern Ossetians.[13] If this 'Dalmatian' Artorius led Sarmatians to victory in Britain, as Littleton and Malcor suggest, could it be that Arthur was originally Roman and the Knights of the Round Table Sarmatians?

Before we turn our attention to Artorius, though, there is an even earlier possibility to explore: that Arthur originated in Ancient Greece. Here our starting point is a bright star by the name of Arcturus in the constellation of Boötes. In Greek Arcturus means 'Bear-ward', reflecting the star's proximity to Ursa Major and Minor (the Great Bear and Little Bear). Greek mythology offers several figures with 'Arthur' type names, the most prominent being Arkas, legendary king of the Arcadians.[14]

Professor Graham Anderson, a specialist in ancient kingship legends, has highlighted parallels between Greek and later Arthurian stories. For example, one tale concerning Arkas mentions the foundation of the city of Trapezous – the name means 'table', which, he suggests, echoes Arthur's Round Table.[15] Another portrays the star Arcturus as a cart-driver carrying a club – a *kalaurops* or *kalabrops*. Could this, he wonders, be the distant origin of Arthur's sword, Excalibur?[16]

These are seductive possibilities but the evidence, on close inspection, is fragile. In Greek, the city-name Trapezous ends in '-zeus', the name of the god who was Arkas's reputed father. That accounts for its inclusion in this story. A city supposedly named for a dining table which was overturned by an irate Zeus has no particular connection with Arthur's Round Table, either in form or function. Excalibur derives originally from the Old Welsh *Caledfwlch*, meaning something like 'harsh-gap', which was then Latinised as *Caliburnus*, and later adapted into French as Excalibur. There is no reason to think that the Greek *kalaurops/kalabrops* in a much earlier text is likely to have influenced this.

Ancient Greek *arktos* and Welsh *arth* both mean 'bear', but this is not so surprising. These are Indo-European languages with many such parallels. Greek was never widely used in Roman Britain and virtually unknown in the post-Roman period among the Britons. While scenes from Greek mythology are not uncommon on villa mosaics in Roman Britain, they probably derive for the most part from standardised pattern books, so are not good evidence for a deep understanding of the subject. There is no evidence that early Greek texts circulated widely in Britain, where even the Greek alphabet was rarely used (generally on imported artefacts) and known only to a few during the Roman period. The Greek connection should be set aside, therefore, as improbable at best and certainly unproven.

Let us therefore turn to the Lucius Artorius Castus commemorated by inscriptions found at Podstrana in Croatia. In the late second century, he served as governor of the province of Liburnia, where he was eventually buried. He had a successful military career, serving as a centurion in Syria, Judea, modern Hungary and Dacia, and then as provost of the Imperial Roman fleet stationed in what is now the Bay of Naples. Thereafter he was prefect of the Sixth Legion, at York, but it is his final military command that has been central to attempts to identify him as the original 'Arthur of Britain'. Unfortunately, the main inscription has split in two and some of the letters have been lost. The critical section reads:

DVCI. LEGG[…]M BRITAN{~I}CIMIARUM
ADVERSUS. ARM[….]S PROCCENTE

How this text is restored is critical. Across the twentieth century Artorius was generally interpreted here as the commander (DVCI – *dux*) of legionary forces from Britain campaigning against the Armoricans (ARM[…]S).

'Armoricans' do not, however, otherwise occur in Roman inscriptions. Neither a tribal nor provincial name, it was used occasionally in Roman literature of tribes centred on Brittany. An otherwise undocumented revolt on this scale seems implausible. 'Commander of British forces' would in any case have been an unusual title at this date. The term *Britannicianae* was normally attached to units which were either raised from, or had distinguished themselves in the conquest of, Britain, rather than to forces stationed there.[17] Such units *are* attested stationed on the Danube and are recorded as having fought against the Parthians in the mid-third century. That offers a more plausible context. Finally, a reading of ARM[....]S in the 1850s, when more of the inscription may have been visible, has an 'E' following the 'M'. If this is correct, 'Armoricans' is impossible; rather, it most probably refers to 'Armenians'.

The alternative therefore is to read this as 'commander of British forces against the Armenians'. In this case 'British' indicates the region where the units were initially recruited and/or their regimental history. Unlike the Armoricans, the Armenians *do* appear on Roman-period inscriptions and there were campaigns of the right period, where the deployment of troops from the Danube frontier makes sense. Most scholars today prefer this second reading. If the 'Dalmatian' Artorius' final posting belonged not to Britain but to Asia Minor, his only command in Britain was his two- or three-year stint as prefect at York. That post would normally have been a quartermaster role, making Artorius poorly placed to have originated the Arthurian legend.

What of the idea that Artorius led a force of Sarmatian soldiers who brought a prototype of the Arthurian stories to Britain? There were certainly Sarmatian troops on the island at this point: Marcus Aurelius had stationed 5,500 men there in AD 175, and there are two inscriptions at Ribchester (Lancashire) pointing to a settlement of veterans in the vicinity in the first third of the third century. Such Sarmatian units may have fought in northern Britain in the Caledonian war concluded successfully by Governor Ulpius Marcellus in 185. But failure to refer to a role in this victorious campaign on his own epitaph must count against any suggestion that Artorius was their commander. Indeed, he was not necessarily even in Britain in 183–85. The evidence for this 'Dalmatian' Artorius as the 'original' Arthur is far from compelling.

What about other theories from antiquity? Parallels have been drawn between later Arthurian stories and tales emanating from the Alan peoples of the Eurasian Steppes. The fourth-century writer Ammianus Marcellinus remarked that the Alans worshipped a sword stuck in the ground, which could have parallels with 'the sword in the stone' of later Arthurian stories.[18] But the Alans were kingless nomads without established ritual sites, and the sword symbolised their god of war. In contrast, the Arthurian 'sword in the stone' served to validate royal succession. Swords were ubiquitous in these societies, so superficial parallels are almost unavoidable; it needs more compelling overlaps than this to demonstrate significant contact.

Similarities have also been noted between Arthurian stories and the so-called Nart Sagas from the Caucasus

– a collection of orally transmitted tales written down only in modern times.[19] Both include duels with giants (in Arthur's case with a giant on St Michael's Mount).[20] Numerous Nart tales feature a magical goblet, Wasamonga, which has been compared with the Grail.[21] Several also refer to magical swords. The Nart hero Batraz has one which has to be thrown into the sea before he can die,[22] recalling Sir Bedivere's disposal of Excalibur in Malory's *Morte d'Arthur*.

The Arthurian stories cannot, however, be read as versions of Nart tales. While a few specific motifs do recur, the stories in which they occur differ markedly. Whereas giants are the Narts' commonest foes, they are rare in Arthurian literature. (Such as there are seem to derive from Welsh storytelling – Olwen's father, for example, was a giant in *Culhwch and Olwen*.) And, while the Narts are sometimes themselves depicted as giants,[23] Arthurian heroes never are. Batraz's sword and Excalibur are thrown into water for very different reasons and with different outcomes.[24] In most other respects, King Arthur and the very un-kingly Batraz differ fundamentally, so it seems implausible to suggest that one derived from the other.[25] The Nart drinking vessel, Wasamonga, distinguishes between truth-tellers and boasters. The Grail first appears as a shallow bowl containing the wafer of the Mass: only later does it evolve into the cup of the Last Supper, a mystical treasure approachable by only the perfect knight. Both Wasamonga and the Grail identify and validate excellence, but Wasamonga operates in a highly competitive, public setting at the feast, to pick out the greatest hero; in contrast, only the most virtuous knight can come into the presence of the Grail and he cannot return to human society, so is lost to the Knights of the Round Table, whose ultimate quest the Grail provides. The contexts are therefore fundamentally different and these differences far outweigh the similarities.

Despite the claims of Littleton and Malcor, the evidence that either Sarmatian or Alan warrior bands drawn into the Roman Empire retained their identities for any length of time is very weak, so the survival of their folklore seems improbable. The legacy of the Alans in Gaul consists of little more than a handful of place names and the popularity of the personal name Alan or Alain, particularly in Brittany. The place names may, of course, derive from the personal name, in which case they offer nothing at all of relevance to the settlement of the Alans as a people. Sarmatians have left even slighter indications of their presence; there are no names of any sort and only a thin scatter of archaeological material. While some of the folk tales told by Alans and Sarmatians could conceivably have been translated into Latin and circulated in Gaul and/or Britain, there is no evidence that this occurred and every likelihood that it did not. There were numerous other groups of barbarian soldiers in Roman employment, none of which left a legacy of this kind. In Britain, Latin was in any case abandoned as a spoken language by around AD 700 in favour of an early form of Welsh, so the window for such a transfer from one language to another was comparatively brief.

In short, it is difficult to imagine that either Greek or Sarmatian/Alan stories ever disseminated in the later

Roman West sufficiently to provide the beginnings of the Arthurian cycle. Some historians write off the potential altogether,[26] but we should not dismiss the possibility of some very limited cross-fertilisation. While similarities between the Nart Sagas and Arthurian stories most probably reflect parallel development, we should not entirely rule out some small-scale links. All three literatures share an Indo-European legacy, so all three might be expected to contain within them some motifs and literary scenes derived from a common, remote past. Arthurian storytelling was active in parts of western Asia from the twelfth century, carried there by crusaders, merchants and missionaries, so some cross-pollination at that stage is also possible. It is, nonetheless, extremely difficult to be sure of any common material.

Only in his name can we have much confidence that Arthur owed a debt to the Continent. The star Arcturus occurs in the book of Job (38:32) and in the seventh-century *Etymologies* of Isidore of Seville. Both were known in early medieval Britain. Latin Artorius is the most likely source of the Celtic personal name Arthur. Confusion with Greek Arcturus seems likely, particularly once Arthur was Latinised in the later medieval period as Arturus. Beyond the name itself, the search for Arthur's origins before AD 500 seems destined, like so much about Arthur's history, to be more intriguing than it is instructive.

3

The Fall of Roman Britain

The ending of Roman Britain is a subject of few facts and many theories. In archaeological terms ... there is a major change detectable between 350 and 450. .... No matter that some level of social continuity can be traced at a few towns and villas, the end date of Britain as part of the empire in 409 looks like a threshold to another sort of world.

David Mattingly, 2006[27]

Map 1: Later Roman and sub-Roman Britain, showing place names referred to in the text

In AD **370**, Britain was a securely held part of the Roman Empire. After 410, it lay outside the empire's defences, exposed to barbarian attack. This is the world we need to bring into focus as we seek to judge whether or not a British 'Arthur' existed. What changed and why?

First, a word about the structure of power in Roman Britain. The late fourth-century diocese of Britain was governed by an official known as a *vicarius*, based in London, responsible to the Gallic Prefecture (in modern France). It comprised five provinces, each with its own governor. The whereabouts of the fifth and last-created (Valentia) is unclear: it may have lain in the north-west, around Carlisle, or perhaps between the Hadrianic and Antonine walls. The other provinces were: Maxima Caesariensis, centred on London; Flavia Caesariensis, run from Lincoln; Britannia Secunda, centred on York; and Britannia Prima, governed from Cirencester. Each province encompassed several tribal territories or *civitates*, which in turn each had an urban centre and some form of municipal government. These towns – and many others – were walled, providing a network of fortified strongholds. However, large parts of northern and central Wales, Lancashire, the Pennines and Cumbria had no local self-government but were administered by garrison commanders.

The structure of society was steeply hierarchical, with civil power in the hands of the major landowning families. To judge by the opulence of the villas they inhabited, their status and wealth reached its peak in the early fourth century. Latin was the language of this elite, of government, culture and trade, though the native Celtic tongue was widely spoken, particularly in the uplands, the countryside and among the lower classes. Christianity was the official religion and was spreading, especially in the towns and wealthier households. By AD 400 Britain had been part of the empire for fifteen generations and its elites were comparatively 'Romanised', though still regarded as 'country cousins' on the Continent.

In the north, the 'General of the Britains' (*Dux Britanniarum*) commanded the Sixth Legion at York and the garrisons south of and along Hadrian's Wall. Marines were stationed around the south-east coast, answerable to the 'Count of the Saxon Shore' (*Comes Litoris Saxonici*) but the senior officer was the 'Count of the Britains' (*Comes Britanniarum*) with a detachment of the field army, probably billeted in towns rather than forts. Another command may have existed in the west, predominantly in Wales, but no such office is recorded. Although many of the inland forts were garrisoned, the island's defences had been adapted to counter the threat of seaborne attack with watchtowers and specialist forts along parts of the North Sea and Irish Sea coasts, as well as the Channel. Barbarian raiding occurred sporadically and sometimes seriously,[28] but until AD 400 attacks were successfully repelled and defences restored.

Civil war posed a greater danger to the unity of the empire. One imperial general, Magnus Maximus, following successes in the north, was proclaimed emperor by his troops in Britain in 385. He led forces to the Continent and enjoyed considerable success, but was eventually killed in 388. Thereafter, Britain's garrison was only restored slowly, and then depleted once more when troops were withdrawn in the late 390s, as threats to the empire mounted elsewhere – and particularly in Italy.

A related problem was army pay. Soldiers were partially paid in kind, receiving foodstuffs and other goods, but money still mattered. Output from the mints of northern Gaul was declining and very few new coins reached Britain after 400. Unpaid, the garrison revolted in 404, proclaiming its support for three different usurpers in rapid succession. The last of these, Constantine III, took most of the troops stationed south of the Humber to Gaul. He had some success in countering barbarian incursions across the Rhine, and briefly secured both Gaul and Spain, but was eventually trapped at Arles and killed.

In the garrison's absence, Saxon raiders seized the opportunity to cross the North Sea. According to the early sixth-century Byzantine historian, Zosimus, the Saxons: 'reduced the inhabitants … to such straits that they revolted from the empire, no longer submitted to Roman law, and reverted to their native customs. The Britons, therefore, armed themselves and ran many risks to ensure their own safety and free their own cities from attacking barbarians.'[29]

Britain had begun to slip from imperial control. The empire no longer had sufficient resources to restore its authority. What did this mean for the Britons? Written sources provide some information. In the late fourth or early fifth centuries, St Patrick was growing up, probably in the west of the country; his father Calpornius was a landowner, town councillor and church deacon, and his grandfather Potitus a priest.[30] Their personal names are Latin, the household was Christian and Patrick's writings show that he had enjoyed a traditional Roman education – until captured by Irish pirates. Such Romano-British gentry were getting on with life much as usual, therefore – notwithstanding barbarian incursions. Patrick's later reference to the sale of his noble status probably means that he sold the family estate, in which case we can infer that a land market was active in the fifth century.

Constantius of Lyon's *Life of St Germanus* describes his hero twice visiting Britain (once was in 429), in response to British requests for assistance in combating heresy. Germanus, the Bishop of Auxerre, preached to British audiences, baptised British soldiers whom he then led against the barbarians, and mingled with high-status Britons. Later, he journeyed to the shrine of St Alban (presumably at Verulamium), where he left relics he had brought with him from the Continent and in return took relics of St Alban back with him to Auxerre.

Gildas, a native Romano-British author writing no later than the early sixth century in high-quality Latin, with access to the Bible and a range of other classical literature, makes references to money, and the ability of contemporaries to finance visits overseas for ordination to the priesthood. Bishops and other clergy are a feature of his work.[31]

These witnesses all suggest that aspects of elite Christian culture survived the early fifth-century crisis. The physical remains, however, tell a very different story. They reveal a dramatic decline in 'Roman' material deposited in Britain, leading archaeologists to view the ending of Roman Britain as a short, sharp shock. Stone, brick and tile fell out of use; no new mosaics or wall paintings were commissioned; trade shrank dramatically; mining ceased; craft production and manufacturing fell away. Because there was so little new material in evidence, fifth-century occupation is difficult to establish on many sites, opening the prospect of widespread desertion. Collapse of the money supply was probably a major factor, undermining markets and the distribution of goods. The shrinking of the military market was also important. Barbarian raids did not precipitate these changes but they certainly accelerated them.

Aspects of this falling-off in material culture had, however, begun long before 400. Urban populations had been shrinking since the second century, leaving large parts of many towns under-used, while product development in the pottery industries had virtually ceased by around 370. The potter's wheel went out of use in the early fifth century, though in some regions pottery was made by hand in much smaller quantities. Older pots were sometimes repaired, noticeably with metal rivets. Most of the best pieces of fifth-century British metalwork, including some fine brooches, come from Anglo-Saxon graves.

Some important sites show signs of continuing use. At St Albans a water pipeline was laid after 450. At Silchester imported pottery, a glass bead and an ogham (archaic Irish) inscription, all demonstrate trading activity into the later fifth century, though the site can no longer be termed 'urban' after 450. 'Black earth', probably from human and animal waste, is often to be found overlying Roman urban levels, so there was some form of continuing occupation – but not the thriving town life of a century earlier.

Numerous hoards of metalwork were buried in the late fourth and early fifth centuries. These may have been deposited for safe-keeping against Saxon raiding, never to be reclaimed, but some may have been ritual deposits, not intended to be recovered. Many come from East Anglia, which was probably the earliest area of Anglo-Saxon settlement. The largest was found near Hoxne (Suffolk) and includes over 5,000 silver coins dating between 395 and 407/8 (and over 12,000 in all). Almost all the coins had been clipped before being buried, a practice which was far commoner in Britain than elsewhere in the empire at this time. The central image is normally preserved in these clipped coins, suggesting an attempt to recover slivers of silver while still leaving money in circulation. Some of the silver was turned into ingots which could be used to pay mercenaries or ransom captives, for example, but some was used to strike new coins, which seem 'official' but are not from established Roman mints on the Continent.

This effort to maintain a coinage system and to manage the supply of silver in Britain suggests that some form of government survived beyond Constantine III. But large sectors of the economy were in terminal decline and such governmental efforts were incapable of providing a permanent solution to the difficulties faced by the British diocese.

Without Roman support, the Britons were forced to look to their own defence. Constantius, Zosimus and Gildas all indicate that, while the Britons had some success in stemming barbarian attacks, they lacked the resources to drive them off permanently. South of the Humber, the withdrawal of troops to the Continent under Constantine left the coasts very vulnerable. In the west, defensive sites such as Tintagel and South Cadbury have yielded pottery imported from the Mediterranean dating to the late fifth and early sixth centuries, so perhaps these places served as refuges for the elite – and ultimately as bases for a new style of British rule, with chieftains or kings emerging from the ranks of the richer aristocratic families.

Further north, troops remained even after Constantine's army left for the Continent in 406. The absence of a landowning and villa-occupying aristocracy in the frontier zone had long left power in the hands of garrison commanders. The northern command structure is unlikely to have survived across the fifth century but there is evidence at Birdoswald, Vindolanda and elsewhere that occupation continued, suggesting the survival of small-scale war bands around Hadrian's Wall until the end of the fifth century.[32] There were also larger British territories in the early sixth century centred on 'native' forts north of the wall, which developed out of the tribes which had long bordered the northern frontier of Roman Britain – including the Votadini in Northumberland and the Lothians, who re-emerge as the Gododdin, and the Damnonii in and around the Clyde Valley, whose name survives in Dumbarton.

The emergence of fifth-century British chieftains and war bands based around defended centres, located in the west and north of the old Roman provinces, provides fertile ground for those wishing to identify a 'real' King Arthur in the decades around 500. Some writers have opted for comparatively localised figures, based for example in the West Country,[33] southern Scotland[34] or the Hadrianic frontier region,[35] with the particular focus tending to shift as academics make progress in developing our understanding of one group of sites then another. Others have preferred a more universal, 'British' hero-figure, a 'king of Britain', uniting for a while much of what had been Roman Britain and marching out repeatedly to defend it from barbarian attack. These are the Arthur figures set in the late fifth or early sixth centuries described and discussed by such post-war figures as Leslie Alcock and John Morris in the 1970s, and more recently by Christopher Gidlow.[36]

The evidence for such an Arthur is in part archaeological, but excavation cannot provide a name; hence, much rests on readings of British literature, predominantly of the ninth and tenth centuries, to which we will turn in later chapters. Both these types of Arthur, the local and the universal, are warrior figures whose activities are framed largely by pressure from barbarian neighbours. It is war against the Saxons – the English if you prefer – which gives this Arthur his *raison d'être*, so it is to the barbarian settlements in Britain that we must now turn.

4

Migration and Settlement

From then on victory went now to our countrymen, now to their enemies: so that in this people the Lord could make trial (as he tends to do) of his latter-day Israel to see whether it loves him or not. This lasted right up till the year of the siege of Badon Hill, pretty well the last defeat of the villains [the Saxons], and certainly not the least. That was the year of my birth; as I know, one month of the forty-fourth year since then has already passed.

Gildas, *The Ruin of Britian*, trans. Michael Winterbottom, 1978[37]

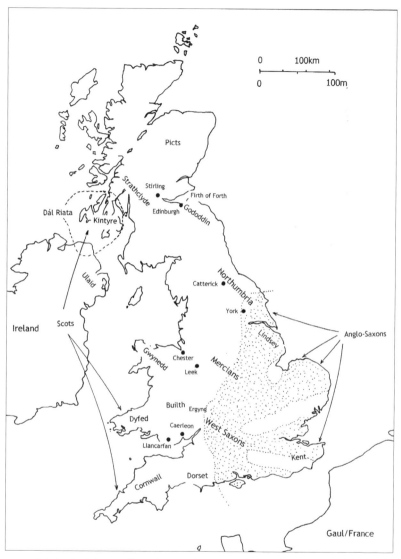

Britain, the Britons and Immigrant Cultures (dotted area signifies the concentration of Anglo-Saxon archaeology pre-550)

With the defences of Britain in disarray, Irish, Pictish and Germanic raiders attacked the old Roman provinces in search of booty and slaves. Some of them stayed. No Pictish settlements have yet been identified by archaeologists anywhere inside Roman Britain, but there is good evidence of Irish spoken in western Wales and in Cornwall. Germanic seafarers – 'Saxons' as they were termed by Roman and British writers – settled in the east of Britain and along the Thames Valley, where widespread archaeological remains have been found.

The key witness now in our quest for Arthur is a Briton (writing in Latin) by the name of Gildas. He composed a work which took the form of an open letter or sermon, entitled *Concerning the Ruin and Complaint of Britain* (*De Excidio et Conquestu Britanniae*).[38] It is the only surviving narrative covering fifth-century Britain to have been written by a near-contemporary. Frustratingly, and perhaps crucially, it does not name Arthur.

Gildas's prime concern was religious (he was later celebrated as an authority on monasticism). *The Ruin* is not a work of history; it is a polemic. For Gildas, the suffering of Britons across the recent past was God's judgment on their erroneous ways; their only hope of divine protection in the future was thoroughgoing moral reform in the present. But the work does feature an extensive historical introduction. This 'historical' section takes as its starting point the Roman conquest of Britain, but for our purposes it is the later passages which matter (chapter numbers are provided in brackets).

Here we read of the wickedness of Magnus Maximus (13). Gildas (mistakenly) sees him as a Briton whose evil campaign against the true emperors has left his land without military defences and cruelly exposed to attack from the warlike Picts and Scots (14). British pleas for help (15) lead to a Roman expedition, which triumphs over the barbarians but then returns home, leaving the Britons to build a turf wall for their own defence. This proves inadequate. The Picts and Scots resume raiding (16). A new plea brings further Roman aid (17) and a repeat of the previous success. This time the Romans organise the building of a stone wall in the north and coastal towers in the south (the Saxon Shore forts), before returning home as before (18). Scottish and Pictish raids resume yet again (19), forcing many Britons to become refugees and causing a famine. The survivors appeal for Roman aid again, to 'Aëtius thrice consul', but on this occasion their entreaties are unsuccessful.

The Britons eventually fight back, freeing themselves temporarily from barbarian attack, but not from their own wickedness (20). Success goes to their heads. Britain is flooded with abundance and corrupting luxury, riddled with drunkenness and vice (21). Divine warnings (including the onset of a terrible plague) that the barbarians will return go unheeded (22). Instead the

Britons convene a council which advises their ruler to hire Saxon mercenaries as protection (23). These duly cross the seas and settle in the east, where they are joined, some time later, by a second, larger force. And then these mercenaries rebel, turn on their hosts, and set about ravaging and devastating Britain 'from sea to sea'.

Many Britons are slaughtered or enslaved. Some manage to emigrate, lamenting (25). Others gather under the leadership of a man called Ambrosius Aurelianus, virtually the only Roman to have survived the storm. He manages to rally forces and together they succeed in inflicting a defeat upon the Saxons. There follows a period of victories and losses (26), as God tests His people 'to see whether it loves Him or not'. The conflict reaches its climax with the siege of Mount Badon (*Mons Badonicus*), described by Gildas as 'pretty well the last defeat of the villains, and certainly not the least'. This would, of course, be one of the battles later assigned to Arthur.

The siege of Mount Badon took place, Gildas records, in the year of his birth, forty-three years and one month previous to the time of his writing. After Mount Badon the cities remain deserted. There are sporadic outbreaks of civil unrest, but no wars with the Saxons. For a while the British leadership is restrained by its experience of the dreadful events which had gone before. As that generation passes, however, a new one takes power, 'slaves of the belly, slaves, too, not of Christ … but of the devil'. In the following chapter (27), using irony for rhetorical effect, Gildas categorises the kings and judges of the present as tyrannical blasphemers before moving on to condemn by name five current rulers in western Britain (28–36), with the priesthood to follow.

Even if we accept the difficulty of reading a narrative that is so polemically religious in its aims, Gildas's account is strewn with factual inaccuracies. The two walls which he dates to a time later than Magnus Maximus (whose campaigns can be dated to 385–88) were both built in the second century. Most of the Saxon Shore forts, on the south coast, were likewise constructed much earlier than his sequence allows. It is difficult to reconcile the two Roman expeditions, which he describes as taking place after Maximus' death (in 388), with what else we know about later Roman Britain. And there are some significant, indeed surprising, omissions from the narrative – particularly the fact that there is no mention of the usurpation of Constantine III. Gildas must surely have been aware of it, since we know that he had read the work of the historian Orosius who is our main source for the first decade of the fifth century and wrote only a few years thereafter.

Most of these inaccuracies lie at the beginning of the period, over a century before Gildas was writing. We can perhaps allow for the fact that he knew little of the history of the northern walls or the Saxon Shore, and therefore fitted them into his account as seemed best. He was probably based somewhere south of the Thames and may not have travelled very much, particularly in light of the fears he expressed about visiting the shrines at St Albans (St Alban, of course) and Caerleon (Saints Aaron and Julius). By the time he reached the arrival of the Saxons, though, we are much closer to Gildas's own lifetime and there is enough detail about the typically 'Roman' ways in which the mercenaries were employed, billeted and supplied for us to have some confidence in his account.

When exactly was *The Ruin* written? Suggestions vary. The consensus among modern scholars is that Gildas is very unlikely to have been writing later than the 540s – and some think the work was composed significantly earlier. But there is no firm proof. What is certain is that we need to be very careful when using it as a source. Gildas's knowledge of events before the lifetime of his parents was poor and his purposes were far from relating historical fact. The 'war of the Saxon federates', which ended around the year of his birth, should, however, be accepted as fact, even if it cannot be exactly dated – nor Mount Badon be definitively located. Arguments have been made in favour of numerous sites, including Bath and its neighbourhood, Badbury Rings and (most recently) Braydon, but there can be no clear favourite as the name does not survive today in a form which is easily recognisable.

This war seems to offer a context for the emergence of Arthur as a British leader fighting the Saxons. Such is the view presented by scholars like John Morris and Leslie Alcock and Christopher Gidlow.[39] They suggest that Arthur might have been a 'Roman-type' commander akin to the *Dux Britanniarum*, who commanded the Roman army of northern Britain, responsible to an insular ruler – or perhaps even that ruler himself. Since Gildas is notoriously unwilling to provide names, the fact that 'Arthur' remains anonymous in the text need not, they argue, mean very much.

Gildas does, however, identify *some* key individuals. He refers to the British ruler who invited in the Saxons as 'the proud tyrant', an epithet which has been interpreted as a play on the Brittonic name, Vortigern (a name which actually occurs in one of the later manuscripts of *The Ruin*, and in Bede's account, which rests on a now lost copy). More certainly, Gildas names the leader of initial resistance to the Saxons as Ambrosius Aurelianus, whom he saw as a 'Roman' figure, rather than a 'British' one. The fact remains: had Gildas named Arthur, we could be confident that he was an historical figure; that he did not necessarily weakens Arthur's claims on history.

How long the war lasted is unclear: some scholars have suggested a period several decades long. The text does not, however, require much time to have passed between the first victory and the last. It is perfectly possible that Ambrosius was still commander at the close of the war. That Gildas refers in the present (in chapter 25) to Ambrosius' grandchildren, over forty years after the victory at Mount Badon, does not require a younger general for the later battles. A mature adult of, say, 50 years old is very likely to have had adult grandchildren known to a writer born in the year of his last significant victory.

The difficulty for us as we search for Arthur is that this Ambrosius cramps the space available for an historical Arthur figure. It is possible to speculate that Arthur and Ambrosius are one and the same person, or, as Geoffrey of Monmouth preferred centuries later, that Arthur was Ambrosius' nephew. But there is no evidence for either of these options. Arthur and Ambrosius share only three letters in common: they are quite different names and there is nothing in any contemporary or near-contemporary record that links them together.

What of the siege of Mount Badon itself? Historians and archaeologists, following Gildas, have generally interpreted it as a resounding British victory which gave the Britons peace and security for a generation or more. But this is an over-simplification of what he actually wrote. Gildas had already referred (in chapter 10) to a 'lamentable division with the barbarians', which suggests a settlement ceding considerable territory to Saxon control. The reference in his preface to a bankrupt aristocracy may even imply tribute payments – or perhaps personal knowledge of elite families evicted from their estates. Gildas's comments are directed primarily at the moral condition of his British 'fellow citizens', but he clearly feared the Saxons in the present. They may not have been on the offensive at the time of writing, but neither had they been expelled or subjugated, and their reach was clearly considerable. Victory was less clear cut than many of Arthur's supporters have wanted to believe. Mount Badon may have been a less decisive triumph than has been assumed. The problem, of course, is that Gildas's audience knew exactly how things stood; it is later readers who struggle to interpret what he wrote.

Archaeology affords us a further perspective on the Anglo-Saxon settlement of Britain. A key source of information is the location of burial remains. By the year 500 there were Anglo-Saxon cemeteries in each of the identifiable Roman provinces (see Map 1). The majority of these graves, however, lay in the east and south-east – in Flavia Caesariensis, where the large cremation cemeteries are concentrated, and in Maxima Caesariensis, where 'Saxon' and 'Jutish' metalwork is in strong evidence. To the west, small numbers of burials have been identified in the upper Thames Valley, on the edges of Britannia Prima, but otherwise the province seems to have been virtually free of Saxon settlement, having to contend instead with mainly Irish colonists. To the north, in Britannia Secunda, early burials seem to be limited to a few cremation cemeteries such as that at Sancton on the Wolds, east of York. These latter two provinces seem to have remained comparatively free of Anglo-Saxon settlement well into the sixth century. Perhaps British resistance was stronger in the north and west. Alternatively, the Anglo-Saxons, having settled initially in and around East Anglia, may have taken time to move outwards from there.

A single British commander ranging widely across the land, countering Saxon raids and attempts at settlement *could* fit both the literary and archaeological evidence, but there are perfectly feasible alternatives – local accommodations and peace treaties, or resistance at the level of province or *civitas*. These explanations match the available evidence equally well. All that can be said for sure is that there *may* be an 'Arthur-shaped space' in the history of late fifth- or early sixth-century Britain. Equally, there may not – and that, alas, is not saying very much.

5

The Earliest Arthurs

The account of Arthur [in the *History of the Britons*] can be seen as wholly fictional, representing our earliest glimpse of the Arthurian legend. But this legend may well have developed in the previous centuries from a genuinely historical figure, active in the 'Irish' areas of Britain or in Ireland, in the sixth century. This figure... may have been a military hero among Irish elites with British connections..., and possibly also among the Britons.

Ken Dark, 2000[40]

Up to this point, we have to some extent been scene-setting. Now we can really begin to grapple with the written evidence for an Arthur of Britain. The facts are few and the search has to be conducted with care but there are nuggets of information here which are worth examining. The way is hard, though, for this material is variously in Old Welsh, Old Irish or Latin, and in texts of kinds which simply are not written today and need to be approached very carefully indeed.

The name Arthur appears in several early texts deriving from the British Isles. These include: a collection of eulogies in Middle Welsh called *Y Gododdin*; the *mirabilia* ('wonder stories') preserved as part of the early ninth-century *History of the Britons*; the king-list of Dyfed (Pembrokeshire), which survives in eighth- and tenth-century versions; the seventh-century *Life of St Columba*; and the Irish chronicles. Let us review each one to see what it can tell us.

Our starting point must be the (potentially) earliest work, *Y Gododdin*, a collection of stanzas recalling dead British heroes. It survives in two versions in the late thirteenth-century *Book of Aneirin*. Both versions show signs of repeated rewriting, corruption and updating. The original seems to date from the sixth century and derives from what is sometimes referred to as the 'Old North' – i.e. British-speaking southern Scotland and northern England, before the Anglo-Saxon takeover. It was probably an oral composition in origin; when it was first written down is unclear. The eulogies or 'death songs' it contains recall a disastrous attack on Catraeth (probably Catterick in North Yorkshire, Roman *Cataractonium*) by a war band serving the king of the Gododdin, the British tribal kingdom occupying the Lothians and Northumberland.

Arthur appears in only one version and in only one stanza (B38). The quotation that follows is based on the reconstruction and translation of the text by Professor John Koch from the University of Wales Centre for Advanced Welsh and Celtic Studies:

> Arthur, Gorddur
> More than three hundred of the finest were slain.
> He struck down at both the middle and the extremities.
> The most generous man was splendid before the host.
> From the herd, he used to distribute horses in winter.
> He would bring black crows down in front of the wall of the fortified town – though he was not Arthur – amongst men mighty in feats
> in the front of the barrier of alder wood – Gorddur.[41]

The hero remembered here is Gorddur, a generous man among his fellows and a great champion in war. Arthur appears only for purposes of comparison: Gorddur, we are told, is impressive in his efforts to feed the carrion crows with the corpses of his slaughtered enemies – but even he is no match for Arthur.

There has been much debate as to whether or not this verse was present in the sixth-century original. A word with an ending comparable to 'Arthur' is required for the rhyme (the last four lines all end -ür in the original), but other, later features have been detected elsewhere in this stanza. John Koch provides cautious support for an early date, but other commentators have been doubtful.[42] The case for Arthur's authenticity is not helped by this stanza occurring in only one version of the collection.

If, for the sake of argument, we suppose that Arthur *did* feature in the sixth-century original, what does it signify? It implies that his name would have been immediately meaningful to a northern British audience. But it is not clear whether he was an historical figure of the recent past, a heroic figure of the remote past, or a character drawn from widely known myth or legend.

If this passing reference to Arthur was inserted at a later date – perhaps when *Y Gododdin* had already passed to Wales and was being adapted for a new audience – it would owe less to Arthur's fame in the north in the sixth century than to his renown in Wales in the central Middle Ages. We cannot be sure which of these interpretations is more likely, rendering it very difficult indeed to make much use of this single reference to the name as a source of the legend.

What, then, of the *mirabilia* which were included in the early ninth-century *History of the Britons* but probably pre-date that work, if only marginally?[43] These include two tales featuring Arthur. The first one reads:

> There is another wonder in the region which is called Builth. There is a pile of stones there and one stone positioned on top of the heap has the footprint of a dog on it. When he hunted the boar Troynt, Cabal, who was the hound of Arthur the warrior, made an imprint on the stone, and Arthur afterwards collected up the heap of stones under the stone in which was the footprint, and it is called Carn Cabal. And men come and they carry the stone in their hands for the space of a day and a night, and on the next day it has returned to the top of the pile.[44]

This is the earliest surviving reference to Arthur's great boar hunt, which features in much greater detail in the Welsh story *Culhwch and Olwen*, which can be traced back to around 1100.[45] The cairn is at Carn Gaffalt, near Rhayader (Powys), in the small early medieval Welsh kingdom of Builth. This folk tale had apparently evolved in order to explain the name of the cairn (*carn*), using the fact that Arthur's hound was called 'horse' – *cabal* in Welsh. It shows that a legendary or mythological figure called Arthur was known locally by the early ninth century.

The second story follows immediately on the first:

> There is another miracle in the region called Ergyng [Archenfield]. There is there a grave next to a spring, which is called Llygad Amr, and the name of the

man who is buried in the tumulus is Amr; he was a son of the warrior Arthur, and he himself killed him in that very place and buried him. And men come to measure the grave, which is sometimes six feet long, sometimes nine, sometimes twelve, sometimes fifteen. Whatever length you measure on one occasion, you do not repeat that measurement, and I have tried myself. [46]

This second story is also etymological in origin (i.e. its purpose is to explain the name), for the spring is the source of the River Gamber. *Amr* derives from an Old Welsh word meaning 'eye', which, as a source of tears, denotes a spring. Once it had been reinterpreted as a personal name – presumably because of phonological similarities between *Amr* and Arthur – it was necessary to add *Llygad*, also meaning 'eye'. This grave is most probably the Neolithic burial chamber known today as Arthur's Stone, at Dorstone in the Golden Valley of western Herefordshire.

These two wonder stories confirm that tales of Arthur were circulating in the southern Welsh borderlands by the early ninth century, and being used there as a means of explaining place- or river-names. Neither tale is in any sense historical, but they do imply that a wild warrior figure called Arthur was well known, at least locally.

It is interesting to note that the use of personal names is unusual among the *mirabilia*, which generally deal with natural wonders such as the Severn Bore. Only St Illtud is otherwise named in person. He again is a figure from south-eastern Wales, this time the southern coastal plain.

The balance of geographical references in the work overall suggests that the author came from that part of the world – he had after all tested the second of these 'Arthurian' wonder stories in person, by doing the measuring. This suggests that Arthur was a familiar figure from the author's home patch. That he chose to inject a little of his own local folklore from 'back home' into a work written for a king in north-west Wales is not perhaps so surprising.

So a heroic Arthur figure was well known, perhaps in north Britain, certainly in south-eastern Wales. But was he a character from myth or legend, or can we identify any 'real' figures with this name?

We can. One occurs in the genealogy of the kings of Dyfed (centred on Pembrokeshire), known in the Roman period as Demetia.[47] This Arthur is listed as the son of Petr (Peter) and great-grandson of Guortepir – possibly the Vortipor named by Gildas as tyrant of this people. A late fifth- or sixth-century date is possible – though whether this section of the genealogy should be accepted as historical is debatable: the claim that the lineage derives from Constantine the Great and his mother Helen via Magnus Maximus is obvious fiction, and the full genealogy only dates from the tenth century. This section is, however, known to us from a separate eighth-century Irish source, which narrows the chronological gap a little. The names before Guortepir are most probably Irish, reflecting the acquisition of power in south-west Wales by Irish incomers. This 'Demetian' Arthur therefore has strong Irish connections, perhaps even Irish ancestry. It is this figure whom the archaeologist Ken Dark considers the most plausible candidate as the origin of the later Arthur,[48] but as there is nothing surviving beyond his name in much later genealogies it is impossible to apply any real test to this evidence.

Other 'Arthur' figures occur in north Britain. Perhaps the best witnessed is Artúr, son of Áedán mac Gabrán, who was king of the territory known as Dál Riata (reputedly founded by Irish immigrants in Kintyre and neighbouring parts of Scotland) from about 574 to 608. Adomnan's *Life of St Columba*,[49] written late in the seventh century but based on an earlier text, has Artúr killed fighting a people known as the Miathi (a group identified with the Maeatae in Roman histories). The place names Dumyat and Myot Hill, near Stirling, which contain this tribal name, suggest that the Miathi lived around the Forth Valley and the battle is dated in the Irish *Annals of Tigernach* to 596, though not very securely.[50]

The name Artúr occurs again in this same royal family in the next generation, as a son of Conaing, one of Áedán's numerous sons. Perhaps he was named after his dead uncle? These appearances of a British name in an Irish-speaking court are unusual. There is some suggestion that Áedán married a British princess, in which case she might have had some influence in the naming of their offspring. The name Conaing is also foreign in origin, but English rather than British. The historian Richard Barber considered that this Artúr, the son of Áedán mac Gabrán, could be the 'original' Arthur, who was later converted to a more 'British' hero in the retelling.[51] But the case is far from compelling.

Another 'Arthur' occurs in the Irish *Annals of Tigernach*,[52] when Artúr son of Bicor, a Briton, threw the stone which killed Mongán, son of Fiachnae Lurgan. This Fiachnae was king of the Ulaid in north-east Ireland until his death in 626, perhaps even high king of all Ireland and a figure around whom legends developed. Mongán seems to have died the year before his father, probably in battle against the forces of Dumbarton, in which case this Arthur should probably be associated with the Glasgow and Strathclyde area.

Lastly, one of the signatories at the great meeting at Birr, Co. Offaly, in central Ireland, where Adomnán presented his 'Law of the Innocents' to the Irish people in 697, was Feradoch, described as the grandson of Artúr. This implies another Irish Arthur active in the early seventh century. Taken together, only one of the figures in these texts is British: the son of Bicor (though even he occurs in an Irish chronicle). The remainder are in some sense Irish. This suggests that the name Arthur was adopted into Irish naming practices by the late sixth century, particularly among families with interests in Britain. Why this should have occurred is not clear. John Morris assumed that these Arthurs were named after a great British Arthur from a generation or two earlier,[53] but that is only one possibility. An otherwise unknown missionary or high-status refugee from Britain is equally possible, or it may be that this was a 'native' Irish name, as well. We simply do not know. But that it was Irish families rather than British who took up the name rather undermines Morris's theory: Adolf is rarely encountered in Britain as a name given to children born after 1939.

To sum up, on the basis of the small quantity of textual evidence which is currently available we can point to two different groups of Arthurs in early medieval Britain. One occurs in predominantly Irish royal families, on both sides of the Irish Sea, in the later sixth and early seventh centuries. None of these Arthur figures became a great warrior king, though some were kings or the sons of kings and some died in battle. The other group is evidenced in *Y Gododdin* and the *mirabilia*. Here Arthur is a pre-eminent warrior, a huntsman and even a kin-slayer, so a figure outside the norms of contemporary society, best viewed within the boundaries of myth or legend.

These two groups were perhaps connected. The appearances of Arthur in the *mirabilia* occur in a region of Wales and the Marches where Irish names outnumber Welsh ones on fifth- and sixth-century inscriptions. This may imply some link between Irish influence and the popularity of the name. If, however, Arthur's presence was original to *Y Gododdin* before this collection of tales travelled south into Wales, then his brief mention in one of these 'death songs' suggests that he was also well known in a northern British context, even though his name was little used by British royals or clerics. Both groups hint at some earlier Arthur, though whether as a figure of history or of legend remains uncertain. Why the name was popular within Irish families rather than their British contemporaries is very unclear.

This survey of the evidence throws up several possibilities, but we cannot assert with any confidence that we have identified an 'original' King Arthur, or offer any biographical details relevant to the figure of the later stories. It does, though, help us appreciate the knowledge base and cultural background of the author of the *History of the Britons* as he set about writing in the early ninth century; his work was designed to lift the spirits of his British countrymen and spur them on to claim both their future and their past as a people beloved of God.

6

The *History of the Britons*

Somewhat later the struggle with the Saxons seems to have been carried on by the shadowy figure of Arthur, but whether he too was a leader of the official Roman kind, as some think, or whether he was only another 'tyrant' like Vortigern, we cannot really know; and nothing useful can be said about him.

Kenneth H. Jackson, 1953[54]

Early in the ninth century an anonymous cleric in Gwynedd, probably an incomer from the south-east of Wales and, probably again, working for the king of the day, wrote a text which has since become known as the *History of the Britons*. He took the Arthur figure with whom he was apparently familiar from folk tales rooted in what is now the west Herefordshire/Powys countryside and converted him to an historical character. This was still a warrior hero, reminiscent of the man in the *mirabilia* stories, but now Arthur came forth as the great British leader, the glorious victor in the 'war of the Saxon federates'. And he was an explicitly Christian figure.

In our quest for Arthur this marks a crucial moment in the interface between history and legend. Up to this point, he has been a figure of folklore, a marginal presence, shrouded in mystery, whose name was used in various Irish and/or British families. After the *History of the Britons* writers feel justified in dating him, crowning him, making him an all-conquering war leader – and imagining ever more elaborate contexts for his heroic exploits.

The *History of the Britons* was written in 829–30, in the fourth year of the reign of King Merfyn Frych of Gwynedd. Since 825, Mercian power had collapsed across southern England, bringing to an end (for the time being) English attempts to conquer Wales. The West Saxon king, Egberht, emerged as the dominant ruler, briefly making himself king of the Mercians. He was recognised as overlord by the Northumbrians (in 829) and the Welsh (in 830). The *History of the Britons* was, therefore, conceived and written at a moment when there was a major shift of political power in southern Britain, with leadership passing from a kingship bordering Wales to one which was more distant – as seen from the perspective of Gwynedd.

The author used a wide variety of sources. Most were in Latin. None – with the exceptions of Gildas's *Ruin of Britain* and some northern British material (which it is difficult to analyse) dated from before the eighth century. For example, the 'Book of the Blessed Germanus' which the author used, was not the fifth-century, Continental 'Life' but a later, highly imaginative British work. Like Gildas, the author of the *History* was less intent on offering an accurate account of the past than on positioning the Britons as the chosen people of God, the latter-day Israelites. His work looked towards a time when the Britons would recover the island which had been lost to them (in the 380s) through the ill deeds of Magnus Maximus: 'On account of [Magnus Maximus] Britain is occupied by foreign peoples and the citizens driven out, until God aids them.'[55]

Our anonymous author was committed to recalling the times when God *had* aided the Britons against their enemies, thereby signposting His support for the future. There is a prophecy at the very heart of the *History of the Britons* (chapter 42) featuring a contest between a red dragon (for the Britons) and a white dragon (the Saxons). Three times the red is close to defeat, but on each occasion he fights back from the brink, and then finally overcomes and expels the white dragon. The author was anticipating a British revival, led – one presumes – by Merfyn Frych of Gwynedd himself, whose freckles (the meaning of *frych*) suggest that he had red hair. This is not just history: it is a political tract about the present.[56]

Intent on presenting the Britons as God's people, the author refocused Gildas's moral indignation onto Vortigern, the tyrant who had fatally invited the Saxons into Britain. He stresses the paganism, duplicity and barbarity of these Saxons and establishes a series of figures, some priestly, some warriors, as Christian heroes: St Germanus, Vortimer (Vortigern's son), St Patrick (who is compared explicitly with Moses in the text) – and Arthur.

Following Patrick's death, the author introduces Arthur (chapter 56):

At that time the Saxons were increasing in numbers and growing in Britain. After Hengest's death, Octa, his son, came from the northern part of Britain to the kingdom of Kent, and from him are descended the Kentish kings. Then in those days Arthur fought with the kings of the Britons against them but he himself was the commander of battles (*dux bellorum*). The first battle was in the mouth of the river which is called Glein. The second, and third, and fourth, and fifth [were] on another river, which is called Dubglas, and it is in the region of Linnuis. The sixth battle was on a river called Bassas. The seventh battle was in the wood of Caledonia, that is Cat Coit Celidon. The eighth battle [was] in the castle of Guinnion, in which Arthur carried the image of St Mary the perpetual virgin on his shoulders (*humeri*), and on that day the pagans were put to flight, and a great slaughter was upon them through the power of our Lord Jesus Christ and the power of Saint Mary his holy virgin mother. The ninth battle was fought in the city of the legions. The tenth battle was waged on the bank of the river called Tribruit. The eleventh battle occurred on the mountain which is called Agned. The twelfth battle was on the mountain of Badon, in which there fell in one day nine hundred and sixty men from one charge [of] Arthur; and no one slew them except him alone, and in all battles he was the victor.[57]

If this passage is accepted as historically accurate, it provides the British victories which were passed over so briefly by Gildas in his account of the 'war of the Saxon federates', leading up to the siege of Mount Badon. It complements that account and establishes Arthur as the British commander.

The problem is that this is a ninth-century text, written some three centuries after the events it describes. Where did the author find his information? Or is it essentially fiction? It was long thought likely that this battle list derived from a Welsh source. The argument goes as follows: the *humeri* ('upper arms' or 'shoulders') should be considered an improbable place to carry the image of

St Mary, which one might rather expect on a shield. The Old Welsh for shield is *iscuit*, which could at some point have been miscopied as *iscuid* – meaning 'shoulder', later translated into Latin as *humeri*. If that mistake were made, then the original text must have been Old Welsh. Poems of a comparable 'battle-listing' type are known from the early Middle Ages, such as that celebrating the victories of Cadwallon of Gwynedd. If a Welsh poem underlay Arthur's battles, it might even have been near contemporary, making the list potentially historical.

Unfortunately, this ingenious argument consists of several layers of hypothesis. An emblem could be carried on a cloak or tunic as easily as a shield, which surely undermines the whole case.[58] That the Latin name for the seventh battle is explained in Welsh suggests that the source was Latin. Similarly, the shorter battle list provided for Vortimer (chapter 44) provides both the English place name Episford (now lost), and the Welsh alternative Rithergabail. Here the source clearly offered English place names, for which the author provided a Welsh equivalent for his Welsh-speaking audience. So the author was attempting to make material which he had in some language other than Welsh more accessible to a Welsh audience, not the reverse. We must therefore discount the possibility that an early source in Welsh lies behind Arthur's battle list and set aside the entire *iscuit/ iscuid/humeri* argument as implausible.

In fact, the prominence of the Virgin Mary in this passage makes it unlikely that *any* early source existed, irrespective of the language used, since the cult of the

Virgin developed in far distant Rome and was introduced to England no earlier than the 670s. It could not have been adopted by the Welsh before 700, and quite possibly not until after their acceptance of the Roman dating of Easter in the 760s. The two references to the cult of the Virgin Mary in this passage therefore undermine any date of composition very much earlier than the author's own lifetime. If there were a pre-existing text underlying the battle list, it must have derived from the same period as most of the author's other identifiable sources, which came from his own or his parents' lifetimes.

In practice it is at least as likely that this battle list was the author's own composition, his chief inspiration being the Bible. First, Arthur's description as *dux bellorum* parallels the unusual term *dux belli* used of Joshua in the book of Judges. Just as in the Old Testament Moses was followed as leader of the Israelites by the warrior Joshua, so here the explicitly Moses-like Patrick is succeeded by the warrior Arthur. This parallel is reinforced by the twelve battles, which equate with repeated use of twelve in the book of Joshua, including Joshua's numbering of the tribes of Israel and the twelve pebbles picked up as he crossed the River Jordan (Joshua, 3:12; 4:2, 3, 4, 8, 20). Second, the battles are most easily read as collected together from a variety of sources. The battle of Chester, for example – here 'the city of the legions' – was an English victory in Bede's *Ecclesiastical History*, which recurs in the *Welsh Annals* under the year 613 (though it probably occurred around 615). Other battles seem to replicate stories from mythology or from Welsh poetry about quite different heroes.[59] Third, it has been suggested that the names offered here are in an Old Welsh characteristic of the period around 800, but not earlier.[60]

Finally, we should note the way in which the battle of Mount Badon is described. This is the only battle which is historically referenced, appearing in Gildas's account of the later stages of the 'war of the Saxon federates'. But in the *History* it reconnects with the superhuman Arthur of the *mirabilia*. The author ends the passage with a flourish, calling attention to Arthur not just as a commander but as a champion: it is he and he alone who slaughters 960 of the enemy in just one charge. Any sense of Gildas's Mount Badon, which was a siege, is entirely lost. Instead, the 'final battle' of the 'war of the Saxon federates' becomes a personal achievement of a kind characteristic not of history but of legend. This is an Arthur figure comparable with the classical Hercules or the Irish Fionn mac Cumhaill.[61]

At this point the author breaks off from telling the story of Britain from the British viewpoint and switches to the annotated English royal genealogies which make up the remainder of the historical section. The stunning victory achieved by the superhero Arthur at Mount Badon resonates across the remainder of the work, providing an example to be emulated by a British leader of the present.

The simplest explanation of the battle list is that the author of the *History of the Britons* was himself its architect and that he wrote it without any coherent source, collecting together from a variety of pre-existing works, both oral and written, the twelve battles he needed to achieve his preferred Biblical symmetry, then fitting the list within his broader narrative by the use of biblical referencing. If so, this passage tells us nothing about an historical Arthur. It tells us a good deal, however, about how Arthur was being conceived, as a culture hero fighting against incomers, within British intellectual circles in the early ninth century. It is surely significant that Arthur is attested in two local etymological tales recorded by this same author in his *mirabilia*. These are located in a region he had certainly visited, and where he perhaps even originated. It is difficult to avoid the conclusion that his motive for developing Arthur in the main body of the *History of the Britons* connected more with his own personal background than with any certain knowledge of an historical warrior called Arthur from the distant past.

The Arthur we experience here was still very much a soldier, and not yet the king with whom we become acquainted in the centuries to come, but he is already a Christian hero, charging into battle under the protection of both Jesus and the Virgin Mary. This successful warrior figure had obvious attractions for the age of chivalry which was about to dawn across Western Europe.

7

The *Welsh Annals*

Arthur is a man without position or ancestry in pre-Geoffrey Welsh sources.

David Dumville, 1977[62]

Arthur emerges as a figure of history in the ninth-century *History of the Britons*. In the *Welsh Annals*, written in the mid-tenth century, he is set into a chronology for the first time. By 1100, an elaborate narrative in Welsh, conventionally called *Culhwch and Olwen,* has Arthur as a king whose warriors and court serve as the backdrop for a whole series of contests between those seeking to further the marriage of Culhwch, Arthur's cousin, with Olwen, and those who oppose it – primarily her father. Alongside, this *King* Arthur features in several Welsh and one Breton saints' lives written in the eleventh or early twelfth centuries. It is in the central Middle Ages, therefore, that King Arthur really begins to emerge from the world of legend and mythology. Admittedly, his progress is far from smooth and it takes time for many familiar characteristics to appear, but the Arthur we see at the end of this process is recognisable as the figure with whom we are familiar today. What can we learn from these texts about the evolution of the Arthur we have come to know?

The *Welsh Annals,* written almost certainly in Dyfed (Pembrokeshire), very early in the reign of King Owain (*c.* 954–88), provide a brief chronological summary of events from the mid-fifth to the mid-tenth centuries. Here, amongst others, we find entries for the battle of

Mount Badon and for Arthur's death, as follows
(conventional dates in brackets):

[516]: The battle of Badon, in which Arthur carried
the cross of our Lord Jesus Christ for three days and
three nights on his shoulders and the Britons were
the victors.

[537]: The battle of Camlann, in which Arthur and
Medraut fell, and there was a mortality [i.e. a plague]
in Britain and Ireland.[63]

Most scholars agree that the first of these 'Arthurian'
entries derives from the same sources as underlie the
History of the Britons, given its use of the same words
and motifs. If there were no such 'sources', as suggested
above, then it can only have been the *History* itself which
underpinned the *Annals*. This new work is, however, less
hostile to the English than the *History*, reflecting King
Owain's reliance on the Anglo-Saxon court for protection
against his cousins in Gwynedd to the north who were
attempting to conquer Dyfed in the 950s. This Arthur is
therefore a 'Christ-helper' rather than a British champion
slaughtering Saxons.[64] Once again he carries something on
his shoulders, but it is unclear if the cross is meant to be
seen as a symbol, or whether the entire episode should be
read as a parallel with Simon of Cyrene, who bore Christ's
cross for him in the Gospels.

This text provides not only clear dates but also two
important new items of information: that Arthur died in
the battle of Camlann, and that Medraut (who is more

familiar today as Mordred) was also killed. But is any of this material historical?

First, the chronology. Arthur's deeds are quite properly inserted after the death of Patrick in 457 and before the death of Maelgwyn, Gildas's Maglocunus, in 547 (whether or not either of these is correct). Bede's *Greater Chronicle* includes the first victory won by Ambrosius Aurelianus in the period 474–91. Our author may have added to these dates the forty-three or forty-four years attached by Gildas to Mount Badon, producing a time-frame close to 516–37.[65] But the dates offered by the *Welsh Annals* are not internally consistent: Maglocunus was still alive when Gildas wrote in the forty-fourth year after Badon, but the gap here between the battle and the death of Maglocunus is only thirty-one years. Not all these dates can be correct and it seems perfectly possible that none is.

Second, the battle reference. Camlann means 'crooked enclosure'. This name exists in several locations in northern and western Britain,[66] and others have probably been lost. But without corroboration from a source nearer to the date of the event it would be rash to accept the battle as historical. Arthur's death at Camlann fighting against Mordred would later become canonical, but it is not even clear from this entry in the *Annals* that they were on opposing sides. The appearance of two different events in this single entry – first the battle, then a great mortality – is unusual in the early section of the *Annals* and has led to the suggestion that the battle might have been added later to an existing text. We must remember that we do not have the original manuscript, only a copy from around 1100.

As we have already seen, Arthur is hardly present in Welsh literature up to around the year 1000, so the mention of him in the *Annals* is exceptional. He is conspicuously absent even from such staunchly nationalistic works as the tenth-century *Armes Prydein* and only begins to appear regularly in the eleventh and twelfth centuries. It seems likely, therefore, that the *History of the Britons* and then the *Annals* were largely responsible for kick-starting Arthur as a figure of history and a focus for storytelling of various kinds. Let us now turn to some of the relevant texts from this period.

The story of *Culhwch and Olwen*[67] (in Welsh datable stylistically to around the eleventh century but surviving only in a copy from about 1400) has Arthur presiding over a magnificent court at Celliwig (unlocated) in Cornwall. He is the patron and protector of his cousin Culhwch (he oversees the numerous feats necessary to the winning of Olwen as a bride for his cousin), and he is leader of the hunt for the terrible boar, Twrch Trwyth. This Arthur is a great king, and central to much of the narrative action, set up as the kingly figure presiding over the good guys versus the wicked chief giant, Ysbaddaden, Olwen's father. This is a 'literary' work, full of wit, stylised challenges and heroic deeds. It is not an historical account, by any stretch of the imagination. But it does reveal Arthur's court as an appropriate space for the gathering of gods, demi-gods and heroes to confront wickedness, in a fashion which parallels stories from Ancient Greece.

This is not the only connection made between Cornwall and Arthur, for Abbot Herman of Tournai's account of a journey undertaken by some of the canons of Laon (in Picardy, France) from Exeter to Bodmin in 1113 confirms that Arthur was remembered in Cornwall at this time – these visitors were shown his chair and his oven and told that he was popularly believed to be still alive. This is the earliest reference to the notion of the 'once and future king' which emerged strongly later in the same century.

A king by the name of Arthur occurs in several Latin saints' lives. In some (for example, the lives of St Illtud and the Breton St Goeznovius) he is depicted very positively, as a great conqueror presiding over a magnificent court, reminiscent of *Culhwch and Olwen*. In others, by contrast, Arthur is characterised as small-minded, angry and unjust. Such works, including the lives of St Padarn and St Cadog, were written as hagiographies to glorify the saint as church-founder, often in defiance of the challenge to local traditions posed by the Anglo-Norman conquest of South Wales. In these stories Arthur is depicted as the secular authority over whom the saint triumphs. His frequent appearances suggest that these authors valued Arthur because he had greater name-recognition than other early kings. He emerges as *the* 'British' secular authority figure of choice from the past, particularly in texts written for an audience including 'foreign' incomers.

This Arthur as a symbol of royal governance might easily have developed out of his role as a warrior leader confronting the Saxons, but the way he is represented in these early medieval texts says more about the local Welsh princes and folk tales of the time – and the particular needs of these authors – than it does about Arthur's historical veracity.

Accurate or not, these texts were clearly influential. Many features found here occur in later Arthurian literature. They include such key associates as Cai and Bedwyr (later Kay and Bedevere); conflicts with dragons (in the lives of saints Carannog and Efflan); Arthur as the great commander and Arthur as the generous patron of a magnificent court. The diversity of these works speaks to both the varying purposes and the cultural complexity and sophistication of this Celtic intellectual elite. It also hints at a richness of Arthurian oral storytelling at this date. None of these portrayals of Arthur is remotely historical, but they lead us inexorably into the material at the disposal of Geoffrey of Monmouth, the half-Norman fantasist and writer of epic who was primarily responsible for the launch of King Arthur onto the European stage as Britain's major contribution to chivalric culture, just a few decades into the twelfth century.

8

Geoffrey of Monmouth

Moved by his country's plight, Dubricius and his bishops placed the crown of the kingdom on Arthur's head. He was a youth of fifteen, of great promise and generosity, whose innate goodness ensured that he was loved by almost everybody. As newly-crowned king, he displayed his customary open-handedness. Such a crowd of knights flocked to him that he ran out of gifts. Yet a man who combines an upright character with natural generosity may be out of pocket for a short time, but will never be the victim of lasting poverty. Arthur, who was both upright and generous, decided on war against the Saxons, to use their wealth to reward his household retainers.

Geoffrey of Monmouth, c. 1123–39[68]

Geoffrey of Monmouth's *History of the Kings of Britain* was completed between 1123 and 1139.[69] Geoffrey claimed that his work was a translation of an ancient book in Welsh, originally from Brittany, supplied to him by Walter, archdeacon of Oxford (where Geoffrey was based), but this is about as plausible as Tolkien claiming that *Lord of the Rings* was written by hobbits.

Geoffrey's main sources were Gildas's *Ruin*, Bede's *Ecclesiastical History* and the *History of the Britons*, including the *mirabilia*, but he also used a wide variety of other works. He was bent on constructing an historical epic, along the lines of Virgil's *Aeneid* or Livy's *History of Rome*, with the Britons as his collective heroes, descended from the Trojans. He used numerous rhetorical devices and literary deceits to that end, citing Homer as witness to Brutus' foundation of Tours, for example (chapter 19), and Gildas for an argument between Lud and Nennius (chapter 22) – both entirely falsely. Credibility was clearly important to Geoffrey, but historical truth was not.

The *History of the Kings of Britain* takes the story from the fall of Troy, via Brutus' settlement of the Trojan survivors in Britain (formally Albion, uninhabited but for a few giants), through to Cadwaladr (a king of Gwynedd in the seventh century, though here detached from any one locality). In its pages we read of the acquisition, tenure, defence and eventual loss of Britain, structured via the reigns of kings. Very few dates are offered, though Geoffrey does record Arthur's death as occurring in 542. Unsurprisingly, the narrative is rooted in the world in which it was written: in contemporary elite values; in the day-to-day life of the twelfth-century Church (albeit with such imaginative additions as an archbishopric of Caerleon); in contemporary political geography; and in familiar titles and honours. Arthur's court in Geoffrey's imagination reflects the growing popularity of courtly love in the twelfth century.

The *History* offers an awe-inspiring sweep through a brilliantly imagined past which demanded acceptance as reality. Its coverage was intentionally uneven, the narrative focusing on the deeds of particular individuals such as Brutus at the beginning, and Brennius (chapters 35–44), whom Geoffrey retrieved and embellished from Livy's much briefer account. By far the most attention, however, centres on Arthur, which is where Geoffrey's *History* provides the most detail. This is unsurprising, given that Geoffrey himself adopted the bynames Artur and Arturus, both in manuscripts of his main work and when witnessing charters at Oxford – he was clearly a great fan. The whole project was perhaps even conceived as a vehicle through which to tell Arthur's story. He dominates books 9 and 10, and his death does not occur until well into book 11 (chapters 143–78, overall), taking up 23 per cent of the entire work. If we include his immediate forebears, his uncle Ambrosius (based ultimately on Gildas's Ambrosius

Aurelianus) and his father, Uther Pendragon (the name Uther may be simply a version of Arthur), this proportion rises to nearer a third. This 'Arthuriana' is the climax of the work.

Geoffrey's Arthur provides a blueprint for successful and virtuous kingship – albeit one destined to fail in the end, as he succumbs eventually to the 'wheel of fortune' which played such a large role in medieval thinking about birth, life and death. Arthur was 'of great promise and generosity, [his] innate goodness ensured that he was loved by almost everyone'.[70] He was the generous lord of a loyal soldiery. Like a Christian crusader, he vanquished the pagan Saxon invaders of the British homeland. And he achieved supremacy, first over the lesser rulers of the British Isles, then over all others rulers of north-western Europe. Finally, he destroyed the armies of Rome in battle: a just result given the demands for tribute which their ambassadors had delivered with such arrogance at Arthur's great court.

This was King Arthur on an imperial stage, the leader of Western Christendom triumphing over a Roman army raised in the East – again there are overtones of contemporary interest in the Holy Land in this work. While Britons had not played a major role in the First Crusade (1096–99), here was an opportunity to set the record straight by backdating their participation as leaders in the fight against both pagan enemies (the Saxons) and easterners (the Romans). The story of this war is told in depth. Thereafter, with Arthur drawn back to Britain by Mordred's revolt, Geoffrey reverts to the less detailed style used earlier in the work to characterise lesser reigns.[71] The final battles, and the king's exit 'to Avallon to have his wounds tended', are worked through at speed.

Many of the characteristics already attributed to Arthur were accentuated and popularised by Geoffrey. His Arthur is a great Christian leader who carries the Church's insignia on his back (and definitely on his shield) into battle. He is a generous patron of loyal followers; a king who presides over a glorious court; a brilliant general; a champion who single-handedly slaughters hundreds of the enemy, and a man of supreme moral integrity. This is the Arthur of *History of the Britons* writ large and meshed with the king from *Culhwch and Olwen*, his story fleshed out with details, associates and characteristics drawn from elsewhere or introduced for the first time. Merlin now emerges to take over the role of soothsayer from the Emrys/Ambrosius character in the *History of the Britons*. Arthur's conception at Tintagel is new (though whether Geoffrey actually knew that Tintagel had been a Dark Age centre or this was just a lucky guess is unclear). Here, too, Merlin provides important assistance to Uther, providing the herbs by which to disguise him so as to enable him to make love to Igerna (Igraine, Arthur's mother), wife of his enemy, Gorlois of Cornwall. Geoffrey has enormous fun with his story, treating his sources with a cavalier disregard which anyone who knew them would have recognised immediately. Few did. He wrote to entertain at least as much as to fill in the great gaps in those areas of British history where Bede had shone no light.

The period from the early ninth to the mid-twelfth centuries defined Arthur, therefore, creating and setting in motion the cultural colossus which then bestrode the Middle Ages. Including all variants, Geoffrey's work in Latin survives in some 219 manuscripts, a mark of its huge popularity. What had, up to this point, been a very Celtic Arthur was now launched upon the world stage.

Why did Geoffrey's *History* prove so popular? It was offered initially to an audience which was predominantly Norman-French, many the grandsons of men who had conquered England in 1066. A history which depicted the Anglo-Saxons as evil pagans had considerable appeal for this audience and offered a degree of legitimacy to the Conquest. That it also portrayed the rulers of Britain as empire-builders and crusaders on a European level sustained the Normans' sense of their own destiny, and connected with their conquests not just in Britain but in Italy, Sicily and the Holy Land. Beyond that, Geoffrey's was a brilliant concoction, providing the post-Conquest kings of England with a history as bogus, as rich, as colourful and as downright entertaining as Virgil had provided for Emperor Augustus. This new history had a great deal in its favour: it demanded attention and its message was so welcome among its elite audience that its weaknesses were passed over. Its influence and momentum quickly became unstoppable.

9

Medieval Arthurs

Then King Arthur and King Ban and King Bors, with their good and trusty knights, set on them so fiercely that they made them overthrow their pavilions on their heads, but the eleven kings, by manly prowess of arms, took a fair champaign, but there was slain that morrowtide ten thousand good men's bodies.

Sir Thomas Malory, 1485[72]

Geoffrey of Monmouth's *History* proved the catalyst for a veritable explosion of Arthurian literature across the Middle Ages, in chronicles, verse and prose. The culmination came with Sir Thomas Malory's great work, *Le Morte d'Arthur*. It was the first Arthurian book to be printed,[73] and it became an overnight literary sensation.

Malory wrote much of *Le Morte d'Arthur* in prison. He lived during the Wars of the Roses, when Britain was convulsed by internecine strife. His text betrays contemporary touches: these include mention of Henry V's campaigns in France; Guinevere taking refuge in the Tower of London (Henry VI's prison in 1471); and Mordred's use of cannons against it. The triumph of Henry Tudor over Richard III at the battle of Bosworth in 1485, the same year that William Caxton printed and published *Le Morte d'Arthur*, helped promote the book even further. The Tudors were not the first dynasty to press King Arthur into service, but the weakness of Henry VII's claim to the throne made links between the Tudor court and Arthurian legend virtually obligatory and of exceptional significance.

Malory was able to draw upon a wide range of Arthurian literature for source material. In the 1150s Geoffrey of Monmouth's *History* had been adapted and translated into French by the poet, Wace, working in Normandy under the patronage of Henry II. Wace provided a version of the legend in rhyming couplets, the *Roman de Brut*,[74] named after Brutus, leader of the Trojans. This proved enormously influential. It contained the earliest mention of both the Round Table and Excalibur, Arthur's sword (in French as opposed to Welsh). It also served as the basis for an alliterative verse translation into English[75] by a priest called Layamon, in which the Round Table is even more prominent.

In this way Arthur escaped out of Welsh folklore, Latin hagiography and neo-Classical epic into French and English. In the later twelfth century, the French poet Chrétien de Troyes introduced fresh characters and plots. He had worked for a time at the court of Champagne, where Henry II's stepdaughter was countess, and gave his stories a more 'French' feel: it was Chrétien who first brought in Lancelot (whose name is obviously French), and with it the story of Guinevere's infidelity, plus the romance of Perceval and the Grail.[76] Arthur was still a vital character but no longer central to the action in many of Chrétien's stories, more a framing presence in the background. Instead the action shifted to other members of his court and Arthurian literature started to become a cycle of stories connected together by a common genre, the Round Table and by his presiding authority. We can see the seeds of something broadly comparable already in the Welsh *Culhwch and Olwen*, but it was the elaboration of the underlying themes in French that led to the multi-stranded Arthurian stories we have today.

Three of Chrétien's works (the *Lady of the Fountain*; *Peredur son of Efrawg*; and *Gereint son of Erbin*) are closely related to romances which later became attached to the famous Welsh story-collection, the *Mabinogion*.[77] These are not direct translations, and it is difficult to judge which came first – the Welsh versions or the French. It was Chrétien's poetry, however, written in Europe's most widely spoken vernacular language, which proved the more influential. His compositions stimulated works in Danish, Dutch, German, Icelandic, Italian, Norwegian, Portuguese, Serbo-Russian, Spanish and Swedish, as well as Latin, Welsh, French and English.[78]

The patrons behind these writings also had other interests in Arthur. Wace had developed Geoffrey's brief flirtation with Arthur's 'un-death', commenting that 'he is yet in Avalon, awaited by the Britons'. For the Plantagenet regime in England this was a dangerous notion. It was important to snuff out the hope of a return by Arthur which might stiffen Welsh resistance to the Anglo-Norman takeover. The 'discovery' of the burials of both Arthur and Guinevere at Glastonbury Abbey served such a purpose. The monks, whose monastery had been devastated by fire in 1184, embraced the idea with enthusiasm in the expectation that it would bring in a new stream of revenue. Digging took place in great secrecy, sponsored initially by Henry II and then, after his death in 1189, by Richard the Lionheart. King Arthur's grave was triumphantly revealed in 1191. Gerald of Wales was one of several who recorded the inscription: 'Here in the Isle of Avalon lies buried the renowned King Arthur, with Guinevere, his second wife.'[79]

The twelfth-century historian William of Malmesbury had already come across tales of the apostle Philip founding Glastonbury. Robert de Boron, a French poet of the late twelfth and early thirteenth centuries, brought together the stories of Joseph of Arimathea, the Grail (Christ's cup at the Last Supper), and the Holy Blood captured therein as he hung on the cross. He depicted Joseph carrying the Grail west, into 'the valleys of Avaron' (or Avallon), where Geoffrey of Monmouth had taken his leave of Arthur. Despite Avallon being a French place name (it is a small town in the Yonne district of Burgundy), the monks of Glastonbury enthusiastically promoted such connections.

Multiple Arthurian tales were now in circulation. They were brought together in the early thirteenth century in what was once termed the Vulgate Cycle, now more often referred to as *The Lancelot-Grail*. This is a large and diverse collection of stories running for centuries across a legendary past and closing with the death of Arthur. At the hands of the Cistercian monks who compiled it, Arthur's story took on ever-greater theological significance. Other writers of the thirteenth and fourteenth centuries continued this process. They composed epics centring on Arthur as the noblest of Christian kings presiding over a magnificent court. They reworked many of the same stories and introduced new characters and exploits as they offered their own versions of the patriotic and uplifting narrative known as the 'Matter of Britain' – the long, heroic but ultimately unsuccessful defence of a 'British' Britain in the Dark Ages, against the Saxons – eventually the English.

Arthur retained his appeal for successive medieval monarchs. Edward I was a particular devotee. His lordship of Ireland, conquest of Wales and attempts to subjugate Scotland naturally fuelled his interest in Arthur's 'high-kingship' over the entirety of the British Isles. He and Queen Eleanor presided over a ceremonial reopening of Arthur's tomb at Glastonbury in 1278, commissioned a shrine to Arthur in the church and promoted the cult of Joseph of Arimathea, whose thorn tree remains a feature of the site. In justifying Edward's claim to Scotland at a hearing at Rome in 1301, his representatives claimed Arthurian authority. The Winchester round table, which today hangs in the castle there, is first known to have been used at a royal feast in 1290.

When Edward's grandson Edward III ascended the throne at the age of 14, it drew favourable comparison with Arthur, whom Geoffrey of Monmouth had made a mere year older at his accession. In 1344 Edward considered 'reviving' Arthur's Order of the Round Table, but eventually founded the rather more modest Order of the Garter a few years later, having run out of money in his war against France. King Edward IV exploited his descent from the Welsh princes via the Mortimer family to claim Arthurian descent, reinforcing his otherwise contentious claim to the throne. He even went so far as to proclaim himself the British messiah prophesied at the close of Geoffrey's *History*.

The Middle English romance *Sir Gawain and the Green Knight*, which probably originated as a Celtic folk tale, takes Arthur's court as its setting – though much of the action seems to occur in north Staffordshire. Contemporary histories fully accepted Arthur as an historical figure. In the words of John Capgrave, in a *Chronicle* he dedicated to Edward IV: 'In these dayes was Arthure Kyng of Bretayn, that with his manhood Conqwered Flaunderes, Frauns, Norwey, and Denmark; and, aftir he was gretely wounded, he went into a ylde clopped Avallone, and there deyed. The olde Britones suppose that he is to lyve.'[80]

It was in Edward's reign that Malory wrote his masterpiece. First entitled *The Whole Book of King Arthur and his Knights of the Round Table*, it survives in only a single manuscript – not the original one, alas – and features eight loosely connected stories. These were restructured and edited by Caxton, who preferred a shorter, snappier title for his printed version, hence *Le Morte d'Arthur* which is how it has been known ever since.

Malory's great work is framed by Arthur's life: his conception at Tintagel occurs in chapter 2; he draws the sword from the stone in chapter 5 and is crowned in chapter 7. He is borne away by barge to Avalon in the fifth chapter of the final book, chapter 21. And so the epic ends – but only once Guinevere and Lancelot too have died, bringing the Arthurian circle to a close.

The start of the reign is optimistic: Merlin gives wise counsel; Arthur obtains Excalibur from the Lady of the Lake; wars are won and enemies slain. Then comes the foundation of the Round Table and Arthur's marriage. From the outset, however, his reign is flawed and tragedy is foreshadowed, for Arthur fathers his nemesis, Mordred, by his own half-sister, Morgan Le Fay. Despite Arthur's attempts to kill his infant son (reminiscent of Herod's attempts to slay the child Jesus), Mordred's ambition and vicious treachery eventually prove Arthur's undoing.

Along the way, Malory offers his audience an array of Arthurian stories, drawn from the French and English romances but simplified as narratives and developed for his own purposes, centring on the ideals of knighthood and chivalry. He focuses in particular on Lancelot, but follows numerous other knights from Arthur's court as they ride out on errantry, culminating in the final and greatest of all chivalric ventures – the quest for the Holy Grail. Finally, Arthur's righteous kingdom dissolves into chaos as Guinevere's adultery with Lancelot leads to divisions which so weaken Arthur that Mordred can seize his crown. The work ends with full-scale civil war and the death of all the leading participants – a picture with all too clear a meaning for Malory's contemporaries.

Henry Tudor, a distant descendant of Edward III (through his mother, Margaret Beaufort, a great-granddaughter of John of Gaunt) and long-time exile in Brittany, made his challenge for the crown in 1485. His campaign began in the country of his birth, Wales, and he marched towards England under the banner of the red dragon featured in the *History of the Britons*. The poverty of his ancestral claim to the throne encouraged his supporters to promote his descent from the twelfth-century Lord Rhys (Rhys ap Gruffudd), and thence spuriously back to King Arthur. Henry even named his eldest son Arthur, to emphasise the claim.

Numerous Arthurian genealogies survive which were written in Henry VII's reign. Fewer come from that of his successor, Henry VIII, whose Yorkist blood via his mother reduced his dependence on Arthurian descent. The 'Matter of Britain', nevertheless, remained popular, and it had political value in defending the dynasty as late as the reign of Elizabeth I. Her court enjoyed a range of Arthurian pageants and tournaments. Thomas Hughes's *The Misfortunes of Arthur* was performed for the queen in 1587, and Spenser's *Faerie Queen,* with its cast of Arthurian knights, was published in 1590, earning its author a pension for life from the delighted monarch.

Arthur, it would appear, was everywhere – the very embodiment of virtue and of patriotic pride. Caxton's preface to Malory's heroic publication seemed to sum it up: 'the most renowned Christian king, first and chief of the three best Christian worthies, King Arthur, which ought most to be remembered among us English men before all other Christian kings.'

10

The Fall and Rise of Arthur

I will again presume to guess, that Her Majesty was not displeas'd to find in this Poem the Praises of Her Native Country; and the Heroick Actions of so famous a Predecessor in the Government of Great Britain, as King Arthur.

John Dryden,1691[81]

Arthur fell out of fashion somewhat at the end of the Middle Ages as Renaissance scholars increasingly questioned his historicity. And, as the English Parliament increasingly asserted its power against the Crown, King Arthur began to be replaced as a cultural icon by interest in things Anglo-Saxon, on the (generally tendentious) grounds that English liberties, the common law and systems of representation all sprang from Anglo-Saxon times.

The Hanoverian monarchy of the eighteenth century presided over a country ever more inclined to look to a Germanic past. By the nineteenth century Arthur had virtually dropped out of the history books – though, interestingly, Arthurian themes then re-emerged strongly in literature and art. Two world wars against Germany, and the loss of the British Empire, provided the space in the twentieth century for the revival of Arthur as a national hero. As the twenty-first century reaches into its second decade, he remains a hugely popular figure in books and films.

William of Newburgh had pronounced Geoffrey of Monmouth 'an impudent and shameless liar' as early as the twelfth century and such criticisms never entirely disappeared, but in Britain Arthur was widely accepted as a real historical figure for most of the Middle Ages. Serious doubts emerged, however, in the fifteenth century. In his preface to Malory, William Caxton, himself an Arthurian enthusiast, felt it necessary to reject contemporary views that 'all such books as have been made of him, be but feigned and fables'. The Italian scholar Polydore Vergil was commissioned by King Henry VII to write a history of England supportive of his claim to the throne, but Vergil was so sceptical of the *Brut* tradition that his work remained unpublished until the second half of Henry VIII's reign. By that stage the king's claim to Arthurian descent was less important and Henry's advisers realised that Vergil's presentation of England's kings as independent of Continental authority offered advantages in the quarrel with Rome. Publication finally went ahead in 1534, as the English Reformation took hold – but only in distant, Protestant Switzerland. Even so, Vergil's debunking of Arthur as an historical figure provoked a xenophobic, pro-Arthur, anti-Catholic backlash from sixteenth-century English men of letters, including Bishop John Bale and the antiquarian John Leland.

With the Dissolution of the Monasteries, numerous medieval manuscripts resurfaced from monastic libraries, where they had lain hidden for centuries. Such figures as Sir Robert Cotton established their own collections, liberating the study of the past from the monks. Laurence Nowell effectively initiated the modern study of early medieval England, but his was primarily an Anglo-Saxon past, not an Arthurian one. The great William Camden showed little enthusiasm for Arthur, omitting him from the historical summary in his *Britannia* of 1585, and elsewhere noting his popularity only among 'the vulgar'. At his accession in 1603, pageantry celebrating the event made reference to James I as a second Brutus, but there was little further exploitation of Arthurian rhetoric on behalf of the Crown, and Arthur was gradually excised from the nation's history. Taking advantage of the artistic freedom that resulted, Shakespeare wrote two plays within the *Brut* tradition, *King Lear* and *Cymbeline,* and Thomas Heywood presented his *Troia Britanica* on the stage in 1609. These were the last major Arthurian works to be performed until the Restoration.

Arthur had some value for the Stuarts as a symbol of the new, united Britain, but the 'Glorious Revolution' of 1688 challenged the political philosophy enshrined in royal absolutism in favour of constitutional monarchy. The *Brut* tradition was ill-adapted to these changing circumstances: neither Geoffrey of Monmouth nor Thomas Malory had paid any attention to parliamentary representation. The culture of medieval chivalry had long since died away and gunpowder had rendered obsolete the heroic style of warfare described in Arthurian stories. In these circumstances, Arthur was fast becoming redundant.

Authors began to seek out new heroes from the past to serve their needs. The career diplomat Sir William Temple, for example, focused on William the Conqueror as a precedent for his patron, the Dutch king William III. The memory of King Alfred, first described as 'the Great' in the sixteenth century, was promoted by clerics and lawyers who believed that the origins of Anglicanism,

English naval power and their own present liberties all descended from his Wessex-centred England. Daniel Defoe was dismissive of Arthurian associations in his *Tour through the Whole Island* (1724–26) and David Hume's *History of England* condemned the Arthurian stories as 'fables', reducing Arthur to a Dark Age prince of the Silures tribe in south-east Wales. Though Edward Gibbon believed that Arthur was essentially historical, he devoted no more than a few lines to his deeds in his famous *Decline and Fall of the Roman Empire*. Sharon Turner, in *History of the Anglo-Saxons* (1799–1805), complained that 'the authentic actions of Arthur have been so disfigured by the additions of the minstrels, and of Jeffry [of Monmouth], that many writers have denied that he ever lived.'[82]

Despite scholarly misgivings, however, Arthur regained popularity in the nineteenth century. The first of several new editions of Malory's *Le Morte d'Arthur* appeared in 1816. These were mined for inspiration by several of the great men of letters of the day, including Sir Walter Scott, whose novel *Ivanhoe* popularised numerous Arthurian themes. This work in turn inspired the great Eglinton Tournament, staged on 30 August 1839 at Eglinton Castle (near Kilwinning, Scotland), watched by a crowd estimated at 100,000. This was a conscious attempt to revive medieval chivalry on an epic scale, bringing together aristocrats from across Europe to participate or spectate – at considerable cost to the host, the Earl of Eglinton.

Alfred Lord Tennyson returned to Malory's King Arthur again and again over the course of his long career, as he worked and reworked his great *Idylls of the King*.

He mined both Malory and the *Mabinogion*, which was first translated into English by Lady Guest in 1849. Tennyson invested heavily in the Arthurian tradition, developing the king as the very epitome of royal virtue – blameless and idealistic – and marrying this figure with contemporary ideas concerning evolution and industrialisation. Tennyson's Arthur emerges as a role model for the Victorian elite, whose destiny it was to rule an empire:

> And after these King Arthur for a space,
> And through the puissance of his Round Table,
> Drew all their petty princedoms under him.
> Their King and head, and made a realm,
> And reigned.[83]

There were darker images as well: Merlin is presented as thoroughly dishonest, and contemporary concerns about faith and religious doubt are explored extensively, particularly through the Grail stories. Tennyson's lead was followed by several others, including the Americans Madison Cawein and Edwin Arlington Robinson, both of whom offered new Arthurian poetry. By the end of the nineteenth century, numerous Arthurian plays were also appearing, though early in the twentieth these gave way to films. A new medium had emerged through which large audiences were increasingly able to experience the Arthurian world.

Particularly in works aimed at children, Arthurian stories of the Victorian era were cleansed of much of the sexual and sinful overtones present in the medieval originals. Lancelot's love for Guinevere, for example, becomes chaste admiration. One of the best-loved books on history written for children – named in 2010 by Prime Minister David Cameron as his favourite – is Henrietta Elizabeth Marshall's *Our Island Story* (first edition, 1905), which offers the Arthurian story (in chapter 12), sword in the stone and all:

> 'Hear me,' said Merlin, 'Uther Pendragon had a son. It was told to me that he should be the greatest king who should ever reign in Britain. So when he was born, lest any harm should befall him, he was given into my care till the time should come for him to reign. He has dwelt in the land of Avalon, where the wise faeries have kept him from evil and whispered wisdom in his ear. Here is your king, honour him'.

Numerous artists, including William Dyce, Edward Burne-Jones and Frederick Sandys painted Arthurian subjects in their work, focusing particularly on several of the female characters in Malory, such as Vivien (or Nimue) and Elaine, and such virtuous warriors as Galahad – a popular image of purity at this date. The appearance on a barge at Camelot of the beautiful Elaine, who had died for love unrequited, was painted by Henry Wallis to illustrate a much-admired passage in Tennyson's popular poem. Alfred Kappes provides perhaps the best-known image of Arthur, with a dragon on his helm, receiving his sword from the upstretched hand of the Lady of the Lake. The only other person present is the aged Merlin, huddled in the rear of the boat. The scene is gloomy, the landscape desolate and the monochrome portrayal accentuates the sense of foreboding. Between 1872 and 1877, Edward Burne-Jones painted *The Beguiling of Merlin*, featuring Nimue reading from a spell book, while Merlin lies prone in the forest. Many of these canvases were vast and imposing (*The Beguiling of Merlin*, for example, is 186 x 111 cm). Dante Gabriel Rossetti and his associates decorated the Oxford Union with Arthurian scenes, and such artists as George Frederic Watts – whose canvases included *Sir Galahad* (1862) – were connected socially with Tennyson's circle, as well as the Pre-Raphaelites. Aubrey Beardsley's focus on Arthur, by contrast, was largely to illustrate books, such as his dramatic version of Sir Bedivere casting Excalibur into the water, in the deluxe 1894 edition of *Le Morte d'Arthur*. His Bedivere is a posed, effeminate figure, inside a border featuring vine scroll of a kind found in early Anglo-Saxon Gospels and on carved stones. Beardsley laid down a powerful challenge to the romanticised and largely asexual work of the Pre-Raphaelites, introducing an erotic dimension to such scenes in his dramatic and distinctive style, using swirls of black ink on white paper.

This artistic focus on Camelot chimed with a new interest in Gothic architecture, which dominated so much of the civic and church building of the nineteenth century. It also influenced the emergence of the Arts and Crafts movement, with which Burne-Jones was heavily involved – for example, designing with William Morris the magnificent tapestry, now in Birmingham Art Gallery, of the *Knights of the Round Table Summoned to the Quest by the Strange Damsel*. For Morris and his circle, Arthur, the Gothic revival, and the medieval world more generally, served as an antidote to the dominant nineteenth-century focus on progress, factories and mechanisation. There was widespread enthusiasm for knighthood, heraldry, antiquarian publishing and genealogy, castle-renovation and/or the building of substantial houses in the style of castles, and the display of weapons and armour.

Meanwhile, across the Atlantic, Arthur was taking off in the US as well, never more spectacularly than when Mark Twain mischievously dropped a young American mechanic in the mix with his *A Yankee at the Court of King Arthur* (1889):

> You see, he [Sir Sagramor] was going for the Holy Grail. The boys all took a flier at the Holy Grail now and then. It was several years' cruise. They always put in the absence snooping around in the most conscientious way, though none of them had any idea where the Holy Grail really was, and I don't think any of them actually expected to find it, or would have known what to do with it if he had run across it.[84]

This is a highly comic book but it also made several very serious points, for Twain was using Camelot as an opportunity to satirise the class system, not just in Britain but also in the US (where slavery was one of his targets).

The popularity of Arthur as a cultural phenomenon chimed with and underscored the reinvention of a code of behaviour based on medieval chivalry, respect for 'the fairer sex' and an urge to protect the weak: think of the cry 'women and children first', on the decks of the *Titanic* as it sank in 1912 and passengers were helped into lifeboats. Arthurian ideals of behaviour resonated across Edwardian Britain, the British Empire and the US, promoted by gentlemen's clubs, boys' movements and the elite institutions of education. Enthusiasts included such diverse figures as Henry Rider Haggard, Rudyard Kipling, Arthur Conan Doyle and Oscar Wilde. This was a social elite defined by its birth and breeding, of course, but also by the Arthurian moral code to which it aspired.[85] The popularity of the gentlemanly game of cricket owed a great deal to such ideas and ideals.

Sceptical historians, by contrast, looked increasingly towards Bede and the *Anglo-Saxon Chronicle*. Since Arthur was named in neither he came to be seen as at best an irrelevance and at worst an invention. He was barely mentioned by the mid-century historian John Mitchell Kemble, or even by Charles Dickens in his *A Child's History of England* (serialised 1851–53). The great Victorian scholar William Stubbs accepted Gildas's condemnation of his contemporaries wholeheartedly and assumed a near-total replacement of the 'enervated and demoralized' Britons by a virtuous, thrusting and ambitious Germanic race. In Stubbs's wake, most English historians of the later Victorian age presented the Dark Ages in terms of a war won by the racially and morally superior English, who drove out or exterminated the degenerate and inferior Britons.

Perhaps unsurprisingly non-English historians retained greater interest in Arthur. The Scot, William Skene, considered the Arthur of the *History of the Britons* historical, to be interpreted as a leader active primarily in the north of Roman Britain.[86] Sir John Rhŷs offered two very different Arthurs from a Welsh perspective: one a sub-Roman military commander of British forces, the other a hero belonging to the world of folklore and mythology.[87]

These were minority voices in end-of-the-century Britain. Rhŷs's dichotomy between a 'real' warrior Arthur and a figure of myth or legend did, however, become central to the debate across the twentieth century. In the 1920s the prolific American medievalist Kemp Malone argued that Arthur and Uther (Arthur's father from Geoffrey of Monmouth onwards) were mythological – and probably in origin the same person, given the similarity of the names.[88] As we have seen, he also raised the possibility that the British Arthur may have derived ultimately from the career soldier Lucius Artorius Castus who died in Roman Dalmatia in about AD 200,[89] the first of several scholars to make this connection. In the later twentieth century the 'mythological' case was reframed by Oliver Padel,[90] arguing persuasively that Arthur originated not as a living person but as a mythic invention of the same sort as the Irish figure of Fionn (Fionn mac Cumhaill, or Finn),[91] a hero designed to carry the aspirations of a people.

Sir Edmund Chambers published a book-length study in 1927 entitled *Arthur of Britain*, examining a wide range of different texts and exploring the ways in which Arthur had been developed by successive authors. Cautious of commenting on the historicity of his hero, he nonetheless rejected the purely mythological interpretation. In his view Arthur was a British leader opposing Anglo-Saxon conquests in the Thames Valley – though his survey of Arthurian place names and local tales left him puzzled at their very wide distribution, especially across parts of Scotland never known to have had 'British' (as opposed to Scottish or Pictish) populations.

A more nuanced interpretation was advanced by R.G. Collingwood, whose chapters in the massively influential *Roman Britain and the English Settlements* (first edition 1936) close with Arthur as the final representative of Rome in Britain, attempting to hold back the tide of Saxon barbarity. 'Through the mist of legend that has surrounded the name of Arthur, it is', he commented, 'possible to descry something which at least may have happened.'[92] Collingwood's reputation as the leading scholar of Roman Britain lent authority to his portrayal of Arthur as a cavalry commander in the late Roman tradition. This book served as a core text for students of the subject from the 1930s right up to the 1970s and encouraged the more positivist approaches adopted by post-war scholarship. Readers who later sought justification for their own historical reconstructions found it easy to ignore the cautious manner in which Collingwood had framed this suggestion, taking his 'Roman' cavalry commander as if it were established fact.

But it was the excavation of South Cadbury hill fort, starting in the 1960s, and the monographs published by Leslie Alcock and John Morris in the early 1970s, which took Collingwood's cavalry commander a whole stage further, restructuring the British Dark Ages around an historical King Arthur.[93] Alcock's work was primarily archaeological and he later distanced himself from this Arthur-centred reconstruction of the period as a whole, and South Cadbury in particular. Morris, however, assembled an extraordinary range of sources, mostly Celtic literature of various kinds, as the raw material from which to paint a vividly imaginative picture of Dark Age Britain. To the unwary, his account seems both scholarly and credible. It was certainly a brave attempt to offer a narrative where such was lacking, but in reality its methodological failings are so great as to undermine the entire work, dependent as it is on the assumption that Arthur's career could be reconstructed reliably from literature written as much as six centuries after the supposed events.[94] Collingwood, Alcock and Morris were all deeply influenced by the bloodshed they had witnessed in the world wars, and Morris's work, in particular, reads in places as if it is a commentary on the Second World War:

> Badon was the 'final victory of the fatherland'. It ended a war whose issue had already been decided. The British had beaten back the barbarians. They stood alone in history, the only remaining corner of the western Roman Empire where a native power withstood the all-conquering Germans. Yet the price of victory was the loss of almost everything the victors had taken arms to defend.[95]

For Morris, Arthur provides the very lynchpin of insular history: 'The history of the British Isles is funnelled through the critical years of Arthur's power and of its destruction, for thence came the modern nations. The age of Arthur is the foundation of British history; and it lies in the mainstream of European experience.'[96]

In a rejoinder to both Alcock and Morris, the Celticist David Dumville launched a scathing attack on their misuse of early Celtic literature as unscholarly. He insisted that: 'Arthur [is] a man without position or ancestry in pre-Geoffrey Welsh sources. I think we can dispose of him quite briefly. He owes his place in our history to a "no smoke without fire" school of thought.'[97] History is not, however, well placed to demonstrate a negative, so the matter still remains one of possibilities and probabilities, rather than certainties. This has left the historical Arthur in a kind of limbo: on the one hand disabled from playing a meaningful role in British history, but on the other not excluded with any real confidence. This is unhelpful to the wider public, whose curiosity feeds instead on older, more confident works – such as Morris's, which remains in print – or on the numerous, later and mostly less scholarly studies.

Outside the academic world Arthur retained considerable affection throughout the post-war era. The profoundly patriotic *Badon Parchments*, published by the Poet Laureate John Masefield in 1947, exemplified this. Here the Angles and Saxons come in their numberless hordes – pagan barbarians, slaughtering, raping and maiming – while their much fewer opponents are valiant

Christians and the last representatives of civilisation. The climax comes at Badon, with the Germanic forces on the brink of victory:

> … with a yelling of all the devils in hell, they charged. I saw them pouring over and down like a dirty cascade in flood on to the lines going up to meet them. We all knew that this was to be the end of the filthy business; all the rest had been prelude.

But at the last minute, Arthur saved the day:

> 'It's Arthur and his horse,' a man said. 'He took them clean off their guard and knocked them cold. They are beaten this time: no man could rally them now.'[98]

A very different set of stories, largely written in the run-up to the outbreak of war, was brought together and completed after 1945 by T.H. White as *The Once and Future King* (1958). White's masterpiece was written as a pacifist tract against the use of violence. Merlin serves as mentor to the future king as a child (when he is known as Wart), in the first part, *The Sword in the Stone* (originally published separately as a novel in 1938), showing him how force is justified only when used in an honourable and righteous cause. This in turn was made into a much-loved children's cartoon by Walt Disney in 1963. A last section, not included in *The Once and Future King* in 1958 (though originally submitted for publication in 1941), but eventually published in 1977 as *The Book of Merlin*, depicts Arthur variously turned into an ant and a goose, so experiencing their lives. Here White was commenting on the dominant political systems of the twentieth century, condemning the collective violence of the ants' totalitarianism in favour of the democratic principles running through the flocks of geese. As Lyó-lyok, the young female goose, said: '"To kill each other? An army of geese to kill each other?" She began to understand the idea very slowly and doubtfully, an expression of grief and distaste coming over her face.'[99]

Later novelists engaging with Arthurian themes have generally pursued less weighty and philosophical objectives; most have offered visions of the past which were essentially romantic. These include Rosemary Sutcliff (seven works, 1959–90), and Susan Cooper (*The Dark is Rising* sequence, 1965–77), whose books centre on present-day children who find themselves caught up in ancient conflicts which are ongoing in the modern era, featuring good versus evil, and looking back to an Arthurian past, relics of which still have power in the present:

Well … he was King of England, and he had his knights of the Round Table, Lancelot and Galahad and Kay and all of them. And they fought jousts and rescued people from wicked knights. And Arthur beat everyone with his sword Excalibur. It was good against bad, I suppose, like you said about, in the fairy stories. Only he was real.[100]

Marion Zimmer Bradley wrote the *Avalon* series (1979–2009, continued after her death in 1999 by Diana Paxson), Mary Stewart, *The Merlin Chronicles* (1980–95); and Count Nikolai Tolstoy *The Coming of the King* (1988). Many of these adventures are full of gore, as Bernard Cornwell's *The Warlord Chronicles* (1995–97), when he turned to the battle of Badon (which was finally won in his account by Irish warriors!), but Arthur presides over all: 'Arthur, scourge of the Sais [Saxons], Lord of Britain and the man whose love hurt him more than any wound from sword or spear. How I do miss Arthur.'[101]

By the close of the twentieth century there was an extraordinary wealth of Arthurian material on offer. There was also a deep divide. On one side stood academic historians, who generally felt that Arthur should be excluded from serious studies of the past, or at most allowed a tightly circumscribed and hypothetical role. On the other was ranged the wider public, who were more sympathetic to Arthur's historical reality and wanted to learn more about, and enjoy, this elusive figure. Arthur remained a magnet for writers and filmmakers, keen to manufacture new and ever more 'real' Arthurian fantasies and serve them up for the enjoyment of his voracious fans. Arthur's origins may be lost in the depths of time but he was still grabbing plenty of attention at the close of the second millennium.

11

Arthur Today – and Tomorrow

Whilst it is possible that chapter 56 of the [History of the Britons] reflects, to some extent, the distorted but genuine traditions of a 'historical Arthur', it is at least equally as likely ... [from] the fact that a concept of Arthur as a mystical hero existed from at least the 8th century, that the opposite is true.

Oliver Padel, 1994[102]

The Jerry Bruckheimer film, *King Arthur*, directed by Antoine Fuqua and starring Clive Owen and Kiera Knightley, went on general release in 2004. Billed as 'the heroic true story behind one of history's greatest legends', it offers a version of the 'Dalmatian/Sarmatian' Arthur but transposed from the late second century to the mid-fifth. The film opens with the young Lancelot being reluctantly recruited from Sarmatia for service in the Roman army in Britain. The enemy initially are the Picts of the north (for whom the film coins the term 'Woads'), but the 'Woads' later join with Arthur against their mutual foe, the Saxons.

No Sarmatians were recruited for service in Britain after 410, when Britain slipped from imperial control, nor are any Sarmatians likely to have had such obviously French names as Lancelot. The 'Dalmatian' Artorius belongs well over two centuries earlier. The case for his leading Sarmatians against the Picts, let alone the Saxons, is unproven. No Roman villas have ever been discovered north of Hadrian's Wall, which undermines a major element of the plot. And there is no evidence of a British–Pictish alliance against the Saxons, though there were occasions when Picts, Scots and Saxons co-ordinated attacks on Britain. The presence of Bishop Germanus beside the wall is utterly implausible: he is not known to have had any dealings with either Alans or Sarmatians in Britain, and he does not seem to have journeyed north of St Albans. He certainly cannot have carried instructions from the Roman emperors to their commanders in mid-fifth-century Britain, for there were no such generals and he seems not to have had any contact with the military authorities on the Continent before coming to Britain.

In short, this film is yet another version of the legend – in this case pitched at an American audience. Arthur is more presidential than kingly, a heroic leader confronting terrorism and finding brave allies in that cause. There is more than a whiff of the aftermath of 9/11 in it, of President Bush, Iraq and the 'coalition of the willing'. It says as much about the present age as it does about the Dark Age.

This is not, therefore, an Arthur from history, despite the film's bold claims to truth. It nevertheless provides important insights into the creation of a pseudo-historical process. In the Arthur story we find a multitude of strands, each developed at a particular point to meet the needs of a particular audience. The more modern the authors the richer the range of sources available to them – and the opportunities to select, modify and recombine elements in constructing their own versions. The approach to Arthurian stories of David Franzoni, the writer of the 2004 *King Arthur* film, is not dissimilar to that of Geoffrey of Monmouth 900 years earlier.

Apart from one (possible but very obscure) aside in the *Gododdin*, we have nothing about Arthur written by anyone whose parents or even grandparents were alive when he was reputed to have been living. Some of us may learn a little from our grandparents about what things were like when they were children. Beyond that, the information flow within families is generally poor. The earliest material which seems to tell us anything very much about Arthur belongs to the ninth century – over 300 years after his reputed triumph at Mount Badon.

So there is a yawning gulf between the period when Arthur is popularly believed to have lived and fought, around AD 500, and the first accounts of these events. It is a gap which poses insoluble problems for the historian. The adherents of the various 'historical' Arthur hypotheses may have convinced themselves that their particular version is true, but they cannot all be right. That does not mean that every theory is wrong; it simply means that none is demonstrably correct, or even demonstrably probable. They cannot, therefore, be accepted as history.

We might perhaps go a little further. Most of the current theories regarding the 'original' Arthur are, frankly, improbable. The 'British' Arthur of the Middle Ages is unlikely to have originated from Greek mythology, even though his name may well derive from the ancient world. The 'Dalmatian' Arthur, Lucius Artorius Castus, looks less plausible as a candidate for the 'original' Arthur of Britain than he did in the late twentieth century, since scholarly reappraisal of the main inscription recording his career now favours his final command as being in Eastern Europe and Asia Minor. There is no significant link between the medieval Arthur and late Roman period Sarmatians or Alans, nor between Arthurian literature and the Nart sagas, setting aside the possibility of minor borrowings and perhaps some very remote antecedents. These should now be accepted as discrete bodies of literature, each with its own quite separate origins.

In fact, of course, Arthur need not have been a real person at all, any more than Hercules or Jason or Hector or Achilles. His earliest appearances in the written record are as easily reconcilable with a figure of myth or legend. Was Arthur perhaps even a local Celtic demi-god, of the kind which was so common in Roman Britain at this time? Such an Arthur is a possibility, though that would require some explanation of his apparently Roman name, which seems out of place in Celtic myth. There is not a scrap of epigraphic evidence, but that does not give us a sufficient basis to dismiss this possibility, particularly given the scarcity of Roman-period inscriptions in the area where we first come across Arthur as a folkloric hero, in the Welsh Marches west of Hereford. Once again, we do not have the evidence either to support or refute any particular thesis regarding the origins of Arthur.

The likeliest 'historical' theory, therefore, remains the oldest: that a comparatively successful commander of British forces fought against Saxon incomers, and perhaps others as well, at some point in the later fifth or early sixth centuries. But we cannot be sure. None of the Arthurs we can document from the sixth and seventh centuries fits the bill; and it is odd that they are almost all in some sense or other 'Irish' rather than 'British'. While it is not, of course, impossible that Britain's rulers employed a non-British general, as Roman emperors had often done, we have no way to test such an hypothesis. The Arthur of the ninth-century *mirabilia* may have had Irish roots, but then again he need not. There is no way of knowing.

In the 1950s, Kenneth Hurlstone Jackson remarked, 'nothing useful can be said about [King Arthur].'[103] In the 1960s, Thomas Jones argued that 'it is difficult to say anything precise about the Arthur of history.'[104] Similar conclusions were reached by Thomas Charles-Edwards in 1991, noting that 'there may well have been an historical Arthur', but 'the historian can as yet say nothing of value about him'.[105] As Guy Halsall recently concluded, 'no sane scholar will now argue that there is definitely a "King Arthur" figure in fifth- or sixth-century history about whom anything solid can be said'.[106] There have been dissenters, of course, for there is no universal agreement on the nature of sanity amongst historians, but the degree of scholarly unanimity is impressive.

All of which leaves us in a difficult place. Scholars continue to publish numerous Arthurian texts, works of analysis and commentaries (see Further Reading), but most of these appear in comparatively expensive 'academic' works which do not circulate widely. They are inevitably drowned out by the far louder representations of Arthur (and Merlin, of course) in film, in TV programmes, in popular books and computer games. For King Arthur is well out of copyright and free to the end user!

Every new generation seeks to interpret its own vision of the world by reference to the past. That is what the author of the *History of the Britons* was doing. It is what

Geoffrey of Monmouth was doing; it is what Malory and Tennyson were doing; and T.H. White and Walt Disney; and indeed Monty Python and Antoine Fuqua. An Arthur who embodies current enthusiasms and desires, political views and cultural preferences, will be heard more loudly, and accepted more willingly, than an Arthur constructed without strong contemporary resonances. In important respects, Arthur is always a figure of the present – and the future – more than the past.

King Arthur is not like other giants of history. He is not a figure whose 'real' story we can know from the evidence currently available. But his tale remains one of the most compelling that we have. It is the story, rather than the man, which commands the stage – a story that we all know, in part at least, in whatever version, through whatever medium. It is the Arthur of legend not the Arthur of history who is the giant – even a giant among giants. And the legend is still growing, mutating, captivating – and inspiring.

Notes

1 Twain, Mark, *A Connecticut Yankee in King Arthur's Court* (New York, 1889), the opening lines of chapter 1.

2 Skiena, S. & Ward, C.B., *Who's Bigger: Where Historical Figures Really Rank* (Cambridge, 2013).

3 Morris, J., *Nennius: British History and the Welsh Annals* (Chichester, 1980).

4 Reeve, M.D. (ed.) & Wright, N. (trans.), *Geoffrey of Monmouth: The* History of the Kings of Britain (Woodbridge, 2007), chs. 143–78.

5 Attributed in error to Alanius de Insulis, *Prophetia Anglicana* (Frankfurt, 1603), 22f, as quoted by Loomis, F.R., 'The Oral Diffusion of the Arthurian Legend', in R.S. Loomis (ed.), *Arthurian Literature in the Middle Ages: A Collaborative History* (Oxford, 1959), pp. 52–71, at p. 62.

6 Alcock, L., *By South Cadbury is that Camelot: Excavations at Cadbury Castle 1966–70* (London, 1972).

7 Alcock, L., *Arthur's Britain: History and Archaeology AD 367–634* (London, 1971).

8 Morris, J., *The Age of Arthur* (London, 1973).

9 See Gidlow, C., *The Reign of Arthur: From History to Legend* (Stroud, 2004), p. xiii.

10 Halsall, G., *Worlds of Arthur* (Oxford, 2013), pp. vii–viii.

11 Littleton, C. Scott & Malcor, Linda A., *From Scythia to Camelot* (2nd edn, London, 2000), p. xxxi.

12 Malone, K., 'Artorius', *Modern Philology*, vol. 22 (1925), pp. 367–74.

13 Littleton & Malcor, *From Scythia to Camelot*.

14 Anderson, G., *King Arthur in antiquity* (London, 2004), pp. 27–41, 64–71.

15 Ibid., pp. 32–3.

16 Ibid., pp. 33–4.

17 It is widely accepted that the inscription contains the misspelling Britanicimiarum for Britannicianarum.

18 Littleton & Malcor, *From Scythia to Camelot*, pp. 181–93.

19 Colarusso J., (assembled, trans. and annotated), *Nart Sagas from the Caucasus* (Princeton, NJ, 2002); Colarusso, J., (ed.) *Tales of the Narts: The Ossetian Epic* (forthcoming).

20 Reeve and Wright, *Geoffrey of Monmouth*, ch. 165.

21 Littleton & Malcor, *From Scythia to Camelot*, pp. 209–32.

22 Ibld., pp. 181-93; Colarusso, *Tales of the Narts*, saga 89.

23 As Colurasso, *Nart Sagas from the Caucasus*, sagas 66, 68.

24 Colarusso, *Tales of the Narts*, saga 89.

25 Contra Littleton, C. Scott & Thomas, A.C., 'The Sarmatian Connection: New Light on the Origin of the Arthurian and Holy Grail Legends', *Journal of American Folklore*, vol. 91 (1978), pp. 512–27.

26 As Halsall, *Worlds of Arthur*, pp. 149–51.

27 David Mattingly, *An Imperial Possession: Britain in the Roman Empire* (Oxford, 2006), p. 529.

28 As the so-called 'Barbarian Conspiracy' of 367, when Picts, Scots and Saxons all raided Roman Britain simultaneously.

29 Zosimus, *New History*, trans. R.T. Ridley (Sydney, 1982), book 6, ch. 5.

30 Patrick, 'Confession', in Hood, A.B.E. (ed.), *St. Patrick: His Writings and Muirchu's Life* (Chichester, 1978), ch. 1.

31 Gildas, *The Ruin of Britain*, in Winterbottom, M. (ed.), *Gildas: The Ruin of Britain and Other Documents* (Chichester, 1978).

32 Collins, R., *Hadrian's Wall and the End of Empire* (London, 2012), pp. 161 ff.

33 As Castleden, R., *King Arthur: The Truth Behind the Legend* (London, 2000), which should be read very critically.

34 As Moffat, A., *Arthur and the Lost Kingdoms* (London, 1999), which likewise requires very critical reading.

35 As suggested by Hutton, R., 'The Early Arthur: History and Myth', in Archibald, E., & Putter, A. (eds), *The Cambridge Companion to the Arthurian Legend* (Cambridge, 2009), pp. 33–4.

36 Alcock, *Arthur's Britain*; Morris, *The Age of Arthur*; Gidlow, *The Reign of Arthur*.

37 Winterbottom, *Gildas*, p. 28

38 Ibid.

39 Alcock, *By South Cadbury*; Morris, *The Age of Arthur*; Gidlow, *The Reign of Arthur*.

40 Dark, K.R., 'A Famous Arthur in the Sixth Century? Reconsidering the Origins of the Arthurian Legend', *Reading Medieval Studies*, vol. 26 (2000), pp. 77–95, at p. 93.

41 Based on Koch, J.T., *The Gododdin of Aneirin: Text and Context from Dark-Age North Britain* (Cardiff, 1997), pp. 22–3.

42 As Padel, O.J., *Arthur in Medieval Welsh Literature* (Cardiff, 2000), p. 6.

43 Morris, *Nennius*, pp. 42, 83.

44 Higham N.J., *King Arthur: Myth-Making and History* (London, 2002), p. 87.

45 R. Bromwich and D. Simon Evans, Culhwch and Olwen: An Edition and Study of the Oldest Arthurian Text (Cardiff, 1992).

46 Higham, pp. 88–9, fig. 15.

47 Ibid., p. 215, fig. 32.

48 Dark, 'A Famous Arthur in the Sixth Century?'

49 Anderson, A.O. & Anderson, M.O. (eds), *Adomnan's Life of St. Columba* (Edinburgh, 1990), book 1, chs 8, 9.

50 Charles-Edwards, T. (ed. and trans.), *The Chronicle of Ireland* (Oxford, 2006), vol. 1, p. 118.

51 Barber, R., *The Figure of Arthur* (London, 1972), pp. 29–38.

52 Charles-Edwards, *The Chronicle of Ireland*, vol. 1, p. 133.

53 Morris, *The Age of Arthur*, p. 116.

54 Jackson, Kenneth J., *Language and History in Early Britain* (Edinburgh, 1953), p. 116.

55 Morris, *Nennius*, pp. 25, 65; the translation is the author's own.

56 Higham, *King Arthur*, pp. 119–36.

57 Morris, *Nennius*, pp. 35, 76; the translation from the Latin is the author's.

58 Gidlow, *The Reign of Arthur*, p. 33.

59 Green, T. *Concepts of Arthur* (Stroud, 2007), pp. 30–4.

60 Ibid., p. 23.

61 Padel, O. 'The Nature of Arthur', *Cambrian Medieval Celtic Studies*, vol. 27 (1994), pp. 19–23.

62 Dumville, David, 'Sub-Roman Britain – History and Legend', *History*, vol. 62 (1977), pp. 173–92.

63 Morris, *Nennius*, pp. 45, 85; the translation is the author's own.

64 Higham, *King Arthur*, pp. 198–216.

65 Wiseman, H., 'The Derivation of the Date of the Badon Entry in the Annales Cambriae from Bede and Gildas', *Parergon*, New Series vol. 17, no. 2 (2000), pp. 1–10.

66 Gidlow, *The Reign of Arthur*, pp. 80–4.

67 Bromwich, R. & Evans, D. Simon (eds), *Culhwch and Olwen: An Edition and Study of the Oldest Arthurian Text* (Cardiff, 1921).

68 Reeve & Wright, *Geoffrey of Monmouth*, from the opening chapter, 143, of Book IX, on p. 192.

69 Ibid., p. vii.

70 Ibid., p. 192.

71 Echard, S., 'Geoffrey of Monmouth', in Echard, S., *The Arthur of Medieval Latin Literature* (Cardiff, 2011), pp. 45–66.

72 Matthews, John (ed.), *Sir Thomas Malory, Le Morte D'Arthur* (London, 2000), opening lines of Book XIV.

73 Ibid.

74 Barron, W.R.J. & Weinberg, S.C., *Le Roman de Brut de Wace* (Harlow, 2001).

75 Barron, W.R.J. & Weinberg, S.C., *Layamon's Arthur: The Arthurian Section of Layamon's Brut* (Exeter, 2005).

76 Kibler, W.W. & Carroll, C.W. (intro and trans.), *Chrétien de Troyes, Arthurian Romances* (London, 1991).

77 Jones, G. & Jones, T. (trans.), *The Mabinogion* (London, 1949).

78 Kennedy, E.D. (ed.), *King Arthur: A Casebook* (New York, 2002), p. xiv.

79 Thorpe, L. (ed.), *Gerald of Wales: The Journey through Wales/Description of Wales* (London, 1978), p. 282.

80 Capgrave, J., *Chronicle of England*, ed. F.C. Hingeston (London, 1858), p. 87.

81 Dryden, John, *King Arthur*, quote taken from Summers, M. (ed.), *John Dryden: Dramatic Works* (London, 1931), p. 242.

82 Turner, S., *History of the Anglo-Saxons*, 3 vol. (London, 1799–1805), vol. 1, ch. 3.

83 Tennyson, Alfred, *Idylls of the King*, 1, *The Coming of Arthur* (1869), lines 16-20.

84 Twain, Mark, *A Connecticut Yankee in King Arthur's Court* (New York, 1889); quote taken from the Bantam Book edition (New York, 1981), pp. 45–6.

85 Girouard, M., *The Return to Camelot: Chivalry and the English Gentleman* (London, 1981).

86 Skene, W., *The Four Ancient Books of Wales* (Edinburgh, 1868), pp. 50–1.

87 Rhŷs, J., *Studies in the Arthurian Legend* (Oxford, 1891).

88 Malone, K., 'The Historicity of Arthur', *Journal of English and Germanic Philology*, vol. 23 (1924), pp. 463–91.

89 Malone, K., 'Artorius', *Modern Philology*, vol. 22 (1925), pp. 367–74.

90 Padel, 'The Nature of Arthur'.

91 For whom, see D. Ó hÓgáin, *Fionn Mac Cumhaill: Images of the Gaelic Hero* (Dublin, 1988).

92 Collingwood, R.G. & Myres, J.N.L., *Roman Britain and the English Settlements* (Oxford, 1936), pp. 320–4.

93 Ashe, G. (ed.), *The Quest for Arthur's Britain* (London, 1968); Alcock, *Arthur's Britain*; Morris, *The Age of Arthur*.

94 The most insightful critique of his method was offered by Kirby, D.P. & Williams, J.E.C., 'Review of *The Age of Arthur*, J. Morris', *Studia Celtica*, vol. 10–11 (1975–76), pp. 454–86.

95 Morris, *The Age of Arthur*, p. 114.

96 Ibid., p. 510 (these are his closing words).

97 Dumville, 'Sub-Roman Britain', p. 187.

98 Masefield, J., *Badon Parchments* (London, 1947), pp. 145, 148.

99 White, T.H., *The Book of Merlin* (Austin, TX, 1977), this quote from the Book Club edition, 1978, p. 82.

100 Cooper, S., *Over Sea under Stone* (London, 1965) – the first in her *The Dark is Rising* sequence; the quote is taken from the 1968 edition, published by Puffin, p. 65.

101 Cornwall, B., *Excalibur* (London, 1997); the quote is from the Penguin edition, 1998, p. 135: the 'love' which is referred to here is Arthur's for the unfaithful Guinevere.

102 Padel, 'The Nature of Arthur', p. 7.

103 Jackson, K. H., *Language and History in Early Britain* (Edinburgh, 1953), p. 116.

104 Jones, T., 'The early evolution of the legend of Arthur', *Nottingham Medieval Studies*, 8 (1964), pp. 3-21, at p. 3.

105 Charles-Edwards, T. M., 'The Arthur of History', in Bromwich et al (1991), pp. 15-32, at p. 29.

106 Halsall, *Worlds of Arthur*, p. 9.

Further Reading

Alcock, L., *Arthur's Britain: History and Archaeology AD 367–634* (London, 1971)

Alcock, L., *By South Cadbury is that Camelot: Excavations at Cadbury Castle 1966–70* (London, 1972)

Anderson, G., *King Arthur in antiquity* (London, 2004)

Archibald, E. & Putter, A. (eds), *The Cambridge Companion to the Arthurian Legend* (Cambridge, 2009)

Bromwich, R., Jarman, A.O.H. & Roberts, B.F. (eds), *The Arthur of the Welsh* (Cardiff, 1991)

Colarusso, J. (assembled, trans. and annotated), *Nart Sagas from the Caucasus* (Princeton, NJ, 2002)

Colarusso, J. (ed.), *Tales of the Narts: The Ossetian Epic* (forthcoming)

Echard, S., *The Arthur of Medieval Latin Literature* (Cardiff, 2011)

Fulton, H. (ed.), *A Companion to Arthurian Literature* (Oxford, 2012)

Gidlow, C., *The Reign of Arthur: From History to Legend* (Stroud, 2004)

Green, T., *Concepts of Arthur* (Stroud, 2007)

Halsall, G., *Worlds of Arthur* (Oxford, 2013)

Higham, N.J., *King Arthur: Myth-Making and History* (London, 2002)

Littleton, C. Scott & Malcor, Linda A., *From Scythia to Camelot* (New York, 2000)

Lupack, A., *Oxford Guide to Arthurian Literature and Legend* (Oxford, 2005)

Matthews, J. (ed.), *Sir Thomas Malory: Le Morte d'Arthur* (London, 2000).

Morris, J., *The Age of Arthur* (London, 1973)

Morris, J., *Nennius: British History and the Welsh Annals* (Chichester, 1980)

Reeve, M.D. (ed.) & Wright, N. (trans.), *Geoffrey of Monmouth: The History of the Kings of Britain* (Woodbridge, 2007)

Winterbottom, M., *Gildas: The Ruin of Britain and Other Documents* (Chichester, 1978)

Web Links

www.arthurian-legend.com/more-about/King-arthur-movie.php – Critical review of the 2004 film *King Arthur*, from the *Guardian*

www.bbc.co.uk/history/ancient/anglo_saxons/arthur_01.shtml

– Introduction to the historical problems posed by Arthur, by Michael Wood

en.wikipedia.org/wiki/Culhwch_and_Olwen – General introduction to the Welsh tale, *Culhwch and Olwen*, with an external link to the e-text

en.wikipedia.org/wiki/King_Arthur – General introduction to King Arthur, providing access to numerous further 'Arthurian' pages

en.wikipedia.org/wiki/King_Arthur_(film) – Introduction to the 2004 film, *King Arthur*

en.wikipedia.org/wiki/Sites_and_places_associated_with_the_Arthurian_legend – Annotated listing of places associated with the Arthurian legends

www.gutenberg.org/browse/authors/c#a435 – Online access to the work of Chrétien de Troyes (you can access numerous medieval and early modern 'Arthurian' works via this site)

www.gutenberg.org/ebooks/10472 – Wace's *Roman de Brut*

www.legendofkingarthur.co.uk – Introduction to King Arthur and the legends of the Round Table, giving places related to the legends helpfully divided by region of Britain

www.parliament.uk/worksofart/collection_highlights/british-history/the-legend-of-king-arthur –Illustrations of the Arthurian scenes decorating the Queen's Robing Room, by William Dyce